HOW EXCEPTIONAL
BLACK
WOMEN
LEAD

Unlocking the Secrets to
Phenomenal Success
in Career and in Life

AVIS A. JONES-DEWEEVER, Ph.D.

Published by Incite Publishing Company
PO Box 131 Woodbridge, VA 22194

Printed in the United States of America

Library of Congress Cataloging-in-Publication Data

Jones-DeWeever, Avis A.
How Exceptional Black Women Lead: Unlocking the Secrets to Phenomenal Success in Career and in Life.

ISBN 978-0-9973005-0-5

Dedication

For Grandma Ada…

Though our time together ended much too soon, you left an indelible mark on my spirit and the most beautiful stain on my soul. In my eyes, you will always be the original

Exceptional Black Woman.

Contents

Black Woman Rise

❝ I'm a trailblazing woman. For me, it wasn't important to make history. But it was important to be the first of many. ❞

—Ambassador Suzan Johnson Cook
Former United States Ambassador-at-Large for
International Religious Freedom

B lack women are born leaders. We are the backbone of our communities, key providers in our homes, and over the years, in many ways, we have been the oil in the engine of change that has transformed nations. Yet, too often, our leadership strengths and capabilities are minimized, prematurely compartmentalized, or actively silenced. In spaces of official leadership, we are commonly missing, though clearly in action. We make sure what needs to be done, gets done, but rarely do we take center stage, receive due credit, or assume the mantle of leadership in any formally designated way. No more. Now is the time to own, and fully step into the breadth of our greatness. Now is the time to lead.

Sistahs, we need a paradigm shift—a completely new way of seeing the world and contextualizing our place within it. The time has come for us to move beyond mere acceptance of things as they currently exist. Instead, we must come to a collective understanding that our destiny is bigger than what we now see. Our divine gifts are capable of more than what is commonly offered. But to get more, we must demand more.

Situated squarely within the cultural spaces of both Blackness and womanhood, ours is a history that is largely defined by the provision of labor. As such, we easily slip into the role of "doer." It's what's expected of

> "What if we perceived a world in which we would just as easily expect to lead as to be led?"

us. It's what we know. We're good at it. But it's not enough. What if, instead, we perceived a world in which we would just as easily expect to lead as to be led? What if we demanded our very own space at the top?

As the youngest woman to have served as the top executive of a historic membership organization reaching four million women worldwide, and now, as an entrepreneur who consults, coaches, and trains women throughout the U.S. and internationally, my journey has afforded me the opportunity to come to know and work with Black women leaders who are nothing short of exceptional. From Corporate America to the Halls of Congress, I've witnessed our brilliance, our drive for excellence, and our commitment to making a difference. And through this journey, I've come to believe that we are not only far too few in number, but sadly, we run the risk of falling even further behind. I am convinced that if we fail to change the current dynamic, we may one day look back at this time as a tragic and disappointing pinnacle of our success.

At this precise moment, we stand at a historic crossroads. America has grown increasingly hostile and intransigent when it comes to boldly facing or addressing in any substantive way issues of race. Simultaneously, the nation is experiencing an invigorated push toward expanded leadership opportunities for women. But Black women are far too often left out of the equation. Although Sheryl Sandberg's prescription to just "lean in" has now become a common part of the national vernacular, the truth of the matter is, advancements in women's leadership have almost exclusively taken on a white woman's face. As a result, Black women are ever so slowly, if not purposefully, being squeezed out of our nation's power structures well before we've had the opportunity to firmly take hold of our fair share. But it doesn't have to be this way. With purposeful and consistent individual and collective action, it is within our capabilities to make real a future that includes Black women in leadership positions across every sphere of influence throughout the nation. Without a doubt, it is within our capability to lead.

Shared throughout the pages of this book is the combined wisdom of 70 exceptional Black women leaders along with my personal perspectives garnered from a two-decade career that includes not only executive leadership but also success in the entrepreneurial realm. We've all come together in hopes that you will replicate our success by providing you with the benefit of our lessons learned along the way. Each of us have shown through our individual accomplishments a capacity to not only lead, but to lead with exceptional success. Corporate America? Check. Non-profit leadership? Check. Public service, elected office, pace-setting entrepreneurship? Triple check. Yes, we did that...and you can too! If within you, burns the heart of a leader, and your destiny is yet to unfold, then learn well the lessons that are imparted here, and commit to act. To create a world that is reflective of our greatness within every arena, we need you to make real your greatest ambitions. We need you to take your place at the top!

Letting Go of the Status Quo

All great transformations in life begin with the decision to reject that which is common reality. By picking up this book, you made that decision. You have decided that now is the time to prepare more, demand more, and get more from your career and your life than ever before. But persisting in that desire requires an intentional rejection of circumstances that do not serve the larger vision you have for your life. It requires an unvarnished awareness of both external and internal challenges and the courage to face those struggles in a bold and strategic way.

By now, you may have come to perceive many of the challenges you face as not "challenging" at all, but merely a function of circumstance. As Black women, we've learned over the centuries to make do. We've become masters at taking whatever unfairness life deals us, and persevere anyway. To save our souls from the constant pain of disappointment, we've learned to divest emotionally from that which we believe cannot be changed, particularly if that change is to be for our exclusive benefit, rather than for the advancement of our children or our men. After a while, the challenges of our particular circumstance can become so commonplace, so automatic and reflexive, that they are all but invisible. "It is, what it is," we often say. But it needn't be that way.

The first thing that is necessary to grasp along your leadership journey is the fact that nothing is what it is by mere chance. Everything is whatever it is, for a reason. And if "it" does not serve the vision you have for your future, then you must engage in purposeful action to create change. The question is how? How do you even begin to change circumstances that surround you when the odds suggest you cannot? Where do you find the time or resources that may be needed to create the life that you envision? And most perplexing, when the change you need is beyond that which you personally control, how on earth do you make it come to be?

The exceptional leaders included in this book will uncover these mysteries and more as the pages unfold. But for now, I offer you this one basic truism. It is a principle that has served me well in both my personal and professional journeys in life. And the principle is, quite simply, pain has a purpose.

Producing Change

Over the years I have discovered that when you allow yourself to truly acknowledge and authentically feel an area of extreme discomfort in life, you will find a way to take the steps necessary to produce change. For example, when the deceptive safety of remaining in that quiet space in the background is overcome by the pain of watching others receive praise based on your ideas, then you will begin to summon the courage to speak up and receive the credit that is due. Likewise, when you allow yourself to really feel the discomfort of seeing others advance while you remain firmly in place, you will commit the time and preparation that is necessary to ascend to unseen heights or you will gravitate to other opportunities that will celebrate your talents and allow you to grow. And in your personal life, when you finally face the fact that a relationship is not providing the love and support that you need and truly deserve, then you will take the necessary steps to improve it or remove it.

Historically, it's impossible to deny that the pain and sacrifices suffered by those who for centuries, fought to produce change in this country, ultimately opened doors of opportunity for us that may have otherwise remained closed. While their efforts did not guarantee an easy journey, it did provide a space to enter. And now that we're here, it's our responsibility to advance to the next level. It's our *responsibility* to lead.

> "It's our *responsibility* to lead."

So yes, the pain of our past has the purpose of shaping our future. But for that purpose to unfold, you must be receptive to the message that lies within. If, in the end, facing the discomfort that you reflexively try to deny, ultimately provides the inspiration to do what needs to be done to maximize your potential and create the life that you deserve and desire, then embrace that pain. Recognize it for the change agent that it is, and then act. If you muster the courage to face it, pain can be as valuable to life as the pleasure we all so naturally seek. When used as the catalyst that it was meant to be, today's pain can be tomorrow's new beginning.

Most of us though, spend our lives running away from the risk of discomfort. The pain of disappointment, the sting of embarrassment, that disconcerting feeling that maybe, just maybe, we're not good enough. Each of these examples are experiences that most seek to avoid. But avoidance, more often than not results in a failure to take the risks that are necessary to fulfill our greatest potential. In our zest to avoid unease, we too often rationalize, make excuses, and eventually come to accept that which should never be tolerated.

If instead, you made the decision, right here and right now, to live your life boldly and honestly, and to really feel both the highs and the lows of life, you will amaze yourself with all you can achieve. You will learn that to get where you've never been before, you must first become uncomfortable with where you are now. You must reject both the seduction of satisfaction and the illusion of impossibility. And when you do, you will come to see that despite the very real barriers and structural challenges that every Black woman faces, it is in fact, possible to break through and achieve your wildest ambitions. Others have done it, and so can you.

Carving Your Path to Exceptional Leadership

Hear me, Sistahs. No one. Absolutely no one, achieves their dreams in isolation. And so, as you embark upon your leadership journey, know that encapsulated within these pages is your personal all-star support system. A SistahMind Group of sorts, made up of some of the nation's most exceptional Black women leaders who have each generously contributed of their time and wisdom so that you can experience a more direct route to success.

Here you will find a very deliberate and practical examination of the principles, practices, and mindset of Black women who have each become exceptional leaders. What's provided in the pages that follow is by no means a theoretical exercise. Nor is it an attempt to craft a feminist manifesto which dawns an overtly colorful veneer. Instead, this book represents a collection and distillation of key insider knowledge transferred from one group of stellar leaders to you, the future of Black women's leadership. If you bring to these pages your grit, intelligence, ambition, and drive, and then match those qualities with the information imparted, then you will be well situated for successful development into the leader you were born to be.

This book is divided into three distinct parts, with Part I serving as foundational for all you will subsequently learn. Thus far, you've gathered the importance of actively rejecting a status quo that fails to serve your interests and long-term aspirations. In Chapter 1, you'll gain greater insight into that status quo and a greater understanding of the systemic challenges Black women specifically face within the professional space. You'll also receive a sobering assessment of our level of representation among leaders in a variety of professional environments. If you're at all like me, you'll feel more than a bit of discomfort at all that will be uncovered. With that in mind, it's my hope that you'll draw on that dis-ease as inspiration to create change. If so, this chapter will also share why now is the optimum time for you to begin your leadership journey, and it will begin to prepare you to make the leap.

Chapter 2 provides a deep dive into the particular challenges you will face as you embark upon your leadership journey. Here you'll get a crash course in the science of discrimination. You'll learn about the existence and persistence of unconscious bias, as well as how the legacy of past injustices can linger within you to this day. But even with these challenges afoot, this chapter will prepare you with the insight necessary to not only face unfairness, but to win.

Part II begins by helping you develop your very own "Leadership Mindset," a key component of success. Each of the women interviewed for this book shared a common perspective, a base sense of drive and confidence that foretold their future success years before it came to be. Here, you'll discover these common, core principles and learn how to go about developing the perspectives that will allow you to be ahead of the game from the start.

The rest of this section provides an in-depth focus on the various paths to exceptional leadership. Chapter 4 offers specific guidance on "Cracking the Corporate Code," so as to understand how best to reach your leadership ambitions specifically within the corporate environment. Chapter 5 examines the issue of change leadership and shares how to distinguish yourself as a successful leader in non-profit organizations, religious institutions, as elected officials, or even a movement-leader.

For those who want to make their mark by living their entrepreneurial dreams, Chapter 6 discusses how to distinguish yourself as a leading Sistahpreneur. Here, you'll gain insight on what it really takes to start and grow a successful business and specifically how to make the leap in a way that breeds long-term success.

The third and final section of the book encourages you to examine your life holistically. Let's face it, few professionals approach home life with the same level of attention and *intention* that is reflexively dedicated to their careers. This section challenges you to not fall into that trap. In Chapter 7 you'll gain insight on how to get the love you deserve, better "balance" career and motherhood, or fully embrace and celebrate all the single life has to offer. In sum, this chapter will help you get clear about how to design and obtain that elusive state of "holistic success" in whatever form you choose. Finally, Chapter 8 challenges you to fully own and step into your greatness—the biggest, boldest, baddest version of yourself and all you have to offer the world.

If there's one thing that I know for sure, it is this: all the information imaginable boils down to merely a theoretical exercise unless action follows it. Action moves mountains. It's the undeniable catalyst to change. Therefore, each chapter concludes with an *Exceptional Black Woman Vision and Action Guide*. Here you'll have the opportunity to reflect on lessons learned, envision how you'll apply those lessons to your life, and then determine specifically what actions you will take to make your aspirations real. Now, if it's your preference to keep all of these exercises together as you make your way through the book, just log on to *www.blackwomenlead.com* and download your free *Exceptional Black Woman Companion Journal*. Here you'll be able to keep your lessons learned and action plans all in one easily accessible place. You'll also get more room for reflection and strategy development within this journal than is possible in the limited confines of an end-of-chapter activity. Additionally, you'll receive insights, information, and implementation strategies on an on-going basis so you can apply the lessons found throughout this book to your career and life in a deep and sustainable way.

Ultimately, it's not enough to know how others achieved or what is even within the realm of possibility. What is of greatest consequence is to understand how to *apply* the knowledge you gain so that you can create the life you want to live. It's only through the application of what you learn here will you be able to maximize your potential to achieve leadership success. That's why reflecting, planning, and acting is absolutely essential for you to make the most of the collective wisdom that you now have at your fingertips.

Your Tomorrow Starts Today

As you begin your leadership journey know this—it is within your power to create the life you've imagined. The wisdom shared throughout this book will be of enormous benefit to

> "It is within your power to create the life you've imagined."

you along the way. But the road will not be easy. For us especially, leadership must not only be sought, it must be relentlessly pursued. The quest must be both intentional and unwavering. And even after our best efforts, leadership opportunities are rarely merely given. In the end, they must be earned, over and over again. And finally, they must be grasped.

If you are ready to commit to the actions that are necessary to become the exceptional leader you were meant to be, then claim the future that awaits and begin to carve your path. Now is the time to step into your greatness. Your biggest, boldest, future begins today.

PART I

Your Time is NOW!

CHAPTER 1

Black Women and Leadership: Where We Now Stand

« Equal opportunities aren't as equal for everyone. »

—Dara Richardson-Heron, M.D.
President & CEO YWCA-USA

My mother often tells the story of a day in her childhood that forever changed the trajectory of her life. By all accounts, it was a normal day. It was not unlike any other for a bright, thirteen-year-old girl growing up in the Jim Crow South. On this day, however, her father received a very special visit. He was a friendly acquaintance; a man whose face she'd seen before. More than seventy years later, her memory remains strikingly clear of what transpired next. Her father's voice, bold and resolute, was calm, yet firm, when he relayed quite matter-of-factly, "I didn't raise any daughters to work in a white man's kitchen." With that response, the two men parted, and my mother's path to leadership began.

As 21st Century Black women, ours is a world that offers infinitely more choices and opportunities than were commonly afforded our mothers, grandmothers, and the generations before. Some things, though, remain stubbornly unchanged. As in days gone by, our reality is one in which work is rarely a "choice" to be flippantly turned on or off, wrestled with, or be held up as a badge of honor or even hidden in relative shame. For us, work has been constant, common, ever-present even. No woman's movement was needed to normalize our labor. We've been here from the beginning, and it's here we remain.

Today, as in years past, Black women are the most likely of all women to work.[1] In our homes, we are not only nurturers but very real providers, supporting over half of all Black families in America today.[2] Still, our presence in and commitment to the workforce has garnered only limited professional success. Despite the fact that we are nearly three times more likely as White women to aspire to professional leadership positions and more than twice as likely to already serve as leaders in our communities, we remain exceedingly rare at the top.[3]

With the benefit of neither whiteness nor manhood on which to lean, our path to leadership is especially complex. More often than not, we end up carefully navigating shifting unwritten rules, doing our best to neutralize negative stereotypical assumptions, and making do with consistent, yet painfully obvious exclusions from key professional networks. In the end, far too many of us spend our entire careers perpetually stuck in something akin to an endless maze rather than a clearly defined path to success. We are, in essence, the "double outsiders."[4] We are the women who face not merely a glass ceiling impeding our admission to the highest echelons of leadership and power, but a ceiling said to be made of concrete.[5]

It's not pretty. That much is true. But it needn't stay this way. The world is changing. And fortunately for us, it's changing in our favor.

In less than thirty years' time, the U.S. Census Bureau predicts that America will face a demographic tipping point. For the first time, it's projected that people of color will make up the majority of Americans.[6] At an even more rapid pace, the global economy is shifting. Currently, seven of the world's ten fastest-growing economies are in Africa.[7] These two base facts foretell a future of shifting dynamics around both racial representation and emerging economic power. At the same time, "women's empowerment" has become an increasingly entrenched national and international imperative. Within this context, the particular frame of reference that we, as

Black women, possess, affords us the advantage of a distinct perspective that is especially needed in an increasingly diverse world. But that doesn't mean the doors of opportunity will automatically open to us. Instead, we must prepare, position, and propel ourselves forward, ultimately creating the opportunities the future will most certainly demand.

Black Women in Corporate America

There are few professional spheres in which changing domestic and global dynamics will have a greater impact than within Corporate America. Both local and global markets are increasingly driven by the buying power of women and racially diverse populations. Still, in spite of growing diversity within the customer base, Corporate America remains one of the most challenging environments for women and people of color to make their way to the top. For Black women specifically, the ascent is particularly steep and treacherous.

Throughout the entire history of the Fortune 500, there have been only 15 Black CEOs, and among the fifteen, only one Black woman.[8] Even aside from the ultimate C-Suite, our presence in other leadership positions remain minimal at best. Only five percent of Black Women who work in Corporate America are in managerial or professional positions.[9] For us, it seems, opportunities to lead in any capacity are especially elusive. But the big question is why? What are those factors that make the leadership of Black women so exceedingly rare?

Several organizations have examined this issue at length over the years, and in many respects, they've uncovered a wide range of hurdles that Black women distinctly face. In 2004, for example, Catalyst surveyed over 1,000 Black women in Fortune 1000 companies and found that we commonly face increased scrutiny, consistently have our authority or credibility questioned, and are especially likely to feel an overall lack of "fit" within the workplace. Especially disturbing is evidence suggesting a real dollars and cents connection to colorism at work. Among the Black women questioned here, those who reported having a lighter skin tone and who described themselves as having less "ethnic" features, were ultimately more satisfied with their pay and opportunities for advancement than those with darker complexions.[10]

Black women across the spectrum, though, reported a wide range of common challenges such as the need to battle negative stereotypes, being excluded from critical informal networks, and having difficulty acquiring influential mentors or sponsors. One would like to believe that under such challenging circumstances women of all backgrounds would help one another, but this study suggests that's not always the case. In fact, Black women reported particularly strained relationships with White women whom they perceived as having an advantage in forming close linkages with White men, the primary gatekeepers and power brokers in the corporate world.[11]

This perception seems to be strikingly close to reality as is evidenced by an inquiry performed by the Executive Leadership Council, which found that Black women not only have to carry the added professional burden of fighting against race and gender bias and stereotypes; but also run into difficulty forming strategic relationships with potential sponsors.[12] White male CEOs interviewed for the study confirmed the problem and suggested that it emanates from Black women themselves. From their perspective, the burden to initiate relationships is on us, not the other way around. As one admitted, though he didn't really "know any Black women," he believed that "they should be aware of that fact and work on it," stating quite simply, "The burden is on Black women to figure it out."[13]

While this may be true, a burden also exists on Corporate America to maximize the full potential of its human capital. And as it now stands, most clearly fall well short of figuring that out either, particularly as it relates to the untapped potential of Black women.

The Center for Talent Innovation's 2015 analysis of the issue provides glaring insight on the degree to which Black women's potential, particularly in the corporate space, routinely goes underutilized. We're nearly three times more likely than White women to aspire to leadership (22% vs. 8%) and much more likely to express confidence in our ability to successfully lead (43% vs. 30%). However, we're also more likely to feel stalled in our careers (44% vs. 30%), and nearly half of us (46%) indicate that our ideas routinely go unheard or fail to be acknowledged at all.[14]

Similarly, leanin.org and McKinsey & Co.'s 2015 Workplace Survey uncovered that fully 85% of Black women would like to receive a promotion, a level that surpasses the aspirations of both White women and White men alike (73% and 76% respectively). But despite our overwhelming ambition, we're the most likely of all women to indicate that we've *never* received active assistance from *any* senior-level people to help us achieve our professional goals.[15]

Clearly, it seems that even when we exhibit an overabundance of qualifications, ability, and the willingness to lead, our ambitions are still met with a dearth of opportunities. But we're not alone. With the glaring exception of White men, it seems virtually everyone else is also underrepresented at the top.

Among the nation's Fortune 500 CEOs, fully 91% are both White and male [16] while women of all races make up only 5% of CEOs.[17] This disparity is particularly striking given that women continue to lead men in college degree attainment, earning more than half of all undergraduate degrees and fully 60% of all Master's degrees.[18] Within the Black community, the educational disparity is even greater. Black women hold two-thirds of all Bachelor's Degrees and more than 7 out of 10 Master's Degrees.[19]

But in spite of our educational progress, women across the board remain largely locked out of corporate leadership opportunities. This continuing reality is a sobering check on the notion of full women's equality in the U.S. Just as disturbing is the rarely discussed fact that racial diversity among the few women who have broken through is nearly nonexistent. As it stands now, only two of the nation's 24 women Fortune 500 CEOs are women of color. And among that duo, Ursula Burns, CEO of Xerox, remains the first and only Black woman to have ever held such an appointment. As such, there is greater diversity among male Fortune 500 CEOs than there is among women. Ironically, today's "diversity" in corporate leadership is increasingly a 'white's only' phenomenon, even when neatly packaged within a tasteful pencil skirt.

Although gains for women of all races and people of color of both genders have each been exceedingly slow, in recent years, there's been a keen divergence of fate between the prevalence of White women CEOs and CEOs of color. As recently as the year 2000, there were only four White women who held the position of CEO in a Fortune 500 company.[20] By 2015, that number had increased more than five-fold, to twenty-two.[21] Over that same period, CEO positions held by people of color initially kept pace with the rising trajectory of white women's representation. But starting in about 2008, ironically coinciding with the election of the nation's first Black President, that trend began to decline and has tumbled downward ever since.[22] So much so that by 2015, there were only ten Asian Americans, ten Latinos, and just five African Americans who headed a Fortune 500 company.[23] White women, in fact, now so far out-pace the representation of CEOs of color that their presence alone nearly equals that of all people of color combined.

While calls to diversify corporate leadership rightfully acknowledges the need to increase the representation of both women and people of color in top corporate roles, it's also important to recognize that in the modern context, the fortunes of White women have largely risen while others have either stalled or begun a steep decline. This is the dirty little secret of diversity, American-style. But it's a secret that shouldn't be surprising. In fact, it's a trend that's consistent with the implementation of affirmative action. Quiet as it's kept, White women have been the main beneficiaries of the program, despite the popular belief that the policy primarily advantages Blacks. [24] As these trends have taken hold over the years, the ability of Black women specifically to pierce through at the highest levels have been virtually nonexistent.

If not for the lone, yet stellar example of an Ursula Burns, we would be completely shut out of the CEO ranks of the nation's top corporations. From this glaring reality, it's safe to say that efforts meant to merely increase the representation of women in leadership generally, don't go nearly far enough. True diversification requires purposeful action meant to increase the representation of women of color as a whole and Black woman specifically, not just because it's the "right" thing to do, but because it's good for business.

The research on this is clear. True diversity in business leadership matters. It leads to more effective decision-making, better positioning within the global marketplace, greater innovation, and the ability to reach a wider customer base. It also saves big bucks when it comes to retention issues, as workplace environments reflective of diversity and inclusiveness have turnover rates 20 percent lower than the norm and experience a 12 percent jump in employee productivity.[25]

In an increasingly racially diverse over-arching environment, and one in which purchasing decisions remain largely influenced by women, having leaders who think, look, and can authentically connect with the customer can provide those companies savvy enough to take advantage of them, a significant competitive edge. It provides a rare opportunity to gain market share by expanding into new, or previously underutilized markets, and win over new customers by understanding, identifying with, and meeting heretofore unmet needs. Clearly, women of color are the gateway to the type of innovation that is necessary to drive growth in the marketplace of today and tomorrow. But Black women specifically, are a particularly wise choice given our natural connection to a Black consumer base that is growing, and widely influential.

According to a Nielsen analysis of Black consumers, 2015 represented a "tipping point" in the buying power of Black Americans. Our consumer dollars have grown tremendously over the years and is projected to reach $1.2 trillion in 2016 on its way to $1.4 trillion in 2020. That represents a 275% growth in Black buying power since 1990. A great deal of this expansion, it seems, can be attributed to a large increase in income for affluent Blacks. In fact, in recent years, especially among Blacks earning $100,000 or more, income growth has outpaced that of Whites significantly.[26]

TABLE 1. The Astounding Growth in Black Buying Power
Percent Income Growth, 2005 to 2014

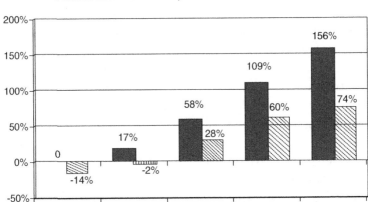

Source: Census Bureau's American Community Survey, Bureau of Labor Statistics as reported by The Atlantic, *Black Consumers Have 'Unprecedented Impact' in 2015.*

Now to be clear, the above illustration does not suggest that Blacks earn more than Whites. Nor does it erase the significant wealth differential between the two groups. But it does indicate an astounding growth in buying power that has no end in sight; particularly as the demographics of the nation continues to shift. Add to this the fact that Black consumers are the largest consumer group of color in the marketplace, are expected to remain so, and tend to be trendsetters for consumers of all races, and the overwhelming importance of the Black buyer becomes exceedingly clear. We not only represent a large and growing segment of consumers, but in many ways we also *define* mainstream culture. As such, we wield tremendous influence over the purchasing decisions of Americans across the spectrum and even consumers all around the globe.[27] Given these facts along with the consistent reality of women driving most purchasing decisions, the need for Black women's leadership specifically within the corporate space is one issue savvy companies can no longer afford to ignore.

Despite this overwhelming imperative, looking forward, there appears to be little to suggest that left to the natural order of things, significant change is forthcoming. The pattern here is clear. Black women are virtually shut-out of corporate leadership opportunities despite our unmatched professional ambition, strong commitment to and consistency within the labor force, and high educational achievements. We're also left behind in spite of our natural connection to an already large, growing, and highly influential segment of consumers. But even with all of these factors weighing heavily on our behalf, for far too many, our race and gender have proven to be quite stubborn barriers to advancement within Corporate America. And as the least likely of all demographic groups to be positioned only one step away from the top spot, [28] without a concerted effort to purposely change the status quo, we will remain the perennial outsider for generations to come.

Black Women in the Non-Profit Arena

Corporate America, though, is not the only space where our representation as leaders is significantly diminished. According to the Philanthropy 400, a list published by the Chronicle of Philanthropy, non-profits too fall short on the issue of diversity at the top.

Among all Philanthropy 400 CEOs, only 19% are women, and just 3.5% are Black.[29] Unfortunately, no data was collected that specifically sheds light on the number of Black women in these positions, but there is little evidence to suggest that the trends found within non-profits would be any different from those discovered within the corporate space. That is to say, women's leadership is most typically a proxy for White women's leadership, just as Black leadership, most often references positions held by Black men. But when looking at race alone, diversity levels within the non-profit arena provide little distinction from that found within the private sector, as fully 94% of Philanthropy 400 CEOs are White.[30]

Despite the dominance of White leadership within the nonprofit space, a survey of 5,000 current or former nonprofit employees found that people of color are more likely than Whites to aspire to one day become a non-profit CEO (40% vs. 32%).[31] Ironically, nonprofit leadership for Whites is less likely to be a professional ambition, but more likely to become a lived reality.

Even smaller non-profits focused specifically on social justice issues largely leave Black women out of formally designated leadership positions. Despite their progressive tendency, many of these organizations perpetuate traditions and organizational cultures that result in either a dearth of leadership opportunities for Blacks (as is the case with women's organizations) or a lack of opportunities for women (as is the case with civil rights organizations). So in spite of the fact that Black women have a history of organizing and activism within both civil rights and women's rights, we typically remain relegated to positions of support, outreach, or implementation, rather than receiving opportunities to lead long-standing traditional organizations.

Now there are a few notable exceptions to this rule. In the women's space, for many years, Faye Wattleton served as President and CEO of Planned Parenthood Federation of America. And today, Teresa Younger serves as the President of the Ms. Foundation for Women, while Dr. Dara Richardson-Heron serves as President and CEO of YWCA-USA. Among civil rights organizations, Sherrilyn Ifill is the President and Director-Counsel of the NAACP-Legal Defense Fund, and Melanie Campbell serves as President and CEO of the National Coalition on Black Civic Participation. But the harsh reality is, each of these women are the exception, rather than the rule.

Largely denied official leadership designations within both traditional civil rights and women's rights organizations, as well as the corporate space, we instead, tend to carve out our own leadership opportunities either specifically within Black women-focused organizations, or as one of many at the helm of new, less formally structured social justice efforts, such as is the case with the Black Lives Matter movement. But perhaps most overwhelmingly, we are choosing to lead our own destiny by answering the call to "be your own boss."

Black Women and Entrepreneurship

Black women are the most likely demographic group in America to start our own businesses. In fact, between 1997 and 2015, the number of companies started by "Sistahpreneurs" grew by 322%, culminating in over 1.3 million businesses nationwide.[32] Together, we generate combined revenues of more than $52 billion.[33] But that doesn't mean that we've escaped the challenges associated with race and gender in the process. If anything, even more intractable barriers begin to come into view.

Though we lead the nation and far outpace other women regarding our tendency to start a business, comparatively speaking, we fall woefully behind when it comes to revenue generation. Our firms, on average, produce just under $40,000 annually, compared to average per-firm revenues of over $68,000 for Latina-owned firms, more than $170,000 for Asian American woman-owned firms, and nearly $190,000 earned by firms owned by White woman.[34] So clearly, merely *owning* a business is not enough. We still have a significant mountain to climb when it comes to maximizing our ability to generate revenue.

Ask any business owner and they'll tell you, in many respects, revenue generation is closely associated with the ability to access capital. It can provide a much-needed bridge during lean times, or be a gateway to growth and even greater levels of profitability. In certain circumstances, it can be that one factor that is the difference between making the dream of entrepreneurship a reality, or simply having that goal become a tragically unfulfilled aspiration. No doubt, capital is key. But like many things in life, access to capital is often not acquired via an even playing field. There are many gatekeepers along the way. And within this environment, we face increased odds of being left behind.

A 2013 study commission by the Small Business Association found that entrepreneurs of color are more likely to rely on their personal wealth rather than outside lenders or investors to start their businesses. If they do attempt to receive a loan, they are more likely to be turned down, even with credit scores and businesses that are similar to Whites. Among those who are successful, they're more likely to pay elevated interests rates. What's worse, these differences in both access to and the overall cost associated with capital acquisition persist years down the line.[35]

For those of us in the high-tech arena, it seems an already bad situation gets even more dire. According to a 2016 examination of

Black women-run tech start-ups, these companies acquired only .2% of venture capital deals, with the average Founder receiving just $36,000 compared to $1.3 million received by *failed* start-ups founded by White men.[36]

So what does this all say about the fate of Black women entrepreneurs? All told, the need to rely on personal wealth, or be locked into elevated interest rates to finance start-up costs or meet business needs, puts us at a distinct disadvantage. We already start off on the wrong side of a wealth gap influenced by not only race but also gender. As a result, the option to tap into personal holdings, for many, is extremely limited, if not virtually nonexistent.

Many do, however, find a way to make their entrepreneurial dreams come true. Perhaps through the use of credit cards, or by borrowing from family and friends, we make it happen. While these small-scale solutions may address an immediate need, in the long run, they result in businesses that start small and typically, stay small over time. As compared to other women business owners, Black women are the most likely to be merely self-employed as opposed to having the capability to also provide employment to others.[37] And it's this capability that is intimately connected to any business' capacity for growth. There is only so much any one person can do. To maximize revenue potential, it's essential that businesses eventually gain the capacity to support additional staff, resulting in greater productivity and potential for revenue growth. Still, over a million Black women have at least made the leap into entrepreneurship. With the proper support, the potential for these businesses to make a difference not only in the lives of each specific business owner but for entire communities, is nothing short of astounding.

Black Women as Public Servants

At local, state, and national levels, Black women are making a difference. We make up the majority of women of color who hold public office[38] and in 2008, the incomparable Michelle Obama made history by becoming the first Black woman to hold the iconic position of First Lady of the United States.

As in other aspects of life, Black women who seek to make a difference through elected leadership, or other forms of public service, face unique challenges. Among those who seek elected office specifically, persistent narrow perceptions of what makes for a viable candidate ultimately means that Black women are often considered to be non-starters by traditional political power brokers.[39] As a result, Black women, as well as other women of color, are much more likely than white women to be actively discouraged from running for political office altogether.[40] Even among those who step up on their own, viability concerns result in less direct support from traditional party mechanisms, resulting in increased difficulty in funding bids for elected office.[41]

For those who make it through this process, once in office, their legislative actions tend to be distinctive, benefitting both women generally and the Black community specifically.[42] Their very presence serves as evidence that it's possible to stand in the face of power and win. The need, though, remains greater than what is currently fulfilled. At the national level, we make up only 18 of the 104 women who serve in Congress, [43] and over a decade ago, we lost the one and only Black woman to have ever had the distinction of serving in the U.S. Senate.[44] However, Congresswoman Donna Edwards along with California Attorney General, Kamala Harris, are both running for the U.S. Senate in 2016, potentially ending the nearly two-decade drought in representation within the more elite of the two national legislative bodies.

In the states, our representation in State Legislatures exceed our representation in Congress. However, we still make up only 2 of the 78 women elected to statewide political offices.[45] We can do better, and we must do better. To ensure our needs and concerns are heard and acted upon in a way that can improve lives broadly and comprehensively, we must have more Black women leaders at every level across the political landscape.

Getting Our Fair Share

So just how do we expand our representation among the nation's leaders? We're already credentialed, capable, and willing to lead, but we remain not only underrepresented but nearly completely off the grid in top positions of leadership in nearly every professional realm. Why does this specific designation remain so elusive for us in particular?

One Harvard Business School examination of the issue suggests that, in essence, Black women are penalized for our ambition.[46] We are, in effect, punished for displaying even the desire to lead. And for those who do make it past this hurdle, other research has found that if our performance is anything less than perfect, we are criticized more harshly than all others who assume the mantle of leadership.[47]

Could it be that because our leadership is so rare, so outside the normal parameters of what most conceive leaders to be, that even our mere aspirations are somehow perceived as illegitimate? Are we somehow thought of as underserved interlopers, seeking to gain entrance to a space in which we clearly "don't belong?" And if, by chance, we do "slip through," even our smallest mistakes are magnified and held up as proof of our pre-conceived illegitimacy?

If this is indeed the case, clearly Black women face an especially tumultuous path to leadership, the overarching dynamics of which are just too daunting to face and systemically change individually. We must instead work together, comprehensively, and strategically to flip the script, so to speak, and change the overarching dynamics that have created the pervasive sense of our leadership illegitimacy in the first place.

Sharing information, lifting up one another, forming strategic networks with the expressed intent of expanding our very own leadership map would be a good place to start. This book represents just one step in that process. But it's an important step. It is specifically with this need in mind that Black women across the professional spectrum agreed to sit down with me to share their wisdom, professional insights, and key insider information so that our prevalence as leaders would grow. We will only break through the wall of exclusion

> "We will only break through the wall of exclusion by pushing through it together."

by pushing through it together. When our prevalence as leaders is no longer a rarity, and instead becomes as common as our representation in the broader population, then in large part, those extra hindrances that we alone face, will slip away, and we will finally be perceived as being precisely where we belong.

Now, of course this change won't happen overnight. In fact, it will be a long and laborious process. But if you're ready to be among the vanguard of a new and powerful cadre of Black women leaders, then now is the time to begin that journey. The future of Black women's leadership begins with you.

The Courage to Lead

It's easy to come away from all that has been shared throughout this chapter feeling more than a little discouraged. Believe me, there are those who are counting on your frustration. It's no stretch to say that millions are personally invested in privileges bestowed and maintained through a status quo that neither serves your interests nor recognizes your capabilities. And even in these days of ostensibly greater levels of sensitivity, or what some might snidely refer to as "political correctness," there are still those who are bold enough to state bluntly the limitations of where they believe you belong.

In December of 2013, The Wall Street Journal published a particularly provocative opinion piece which lamented the doom of WASP domination in America.[48] White Anglo-Saxon Protestants, it argued, are the rightful "ruling class" of the United States. As such, allowing individuals to achieve positions based on their personal qualifications or "merit" rather than by familial heritage, ultimately spells doom for the future of the nation. Yes, even in the modern era, there are still those who think this way. And while most are likely to hold such perspectives close to their chest, that doesn't negate the fact that these feelings still exist. Whether or not they're openly acknowledged or overtly verbalized, they can still, at times, be the base motivation for those who object to notions of expanding leadership opportunities beyond the WASP (and male) status quo.

While this truth is undeniable, it's also true that there exist people of good will who understand and are personally invested in the concept of fairness and meritorious ascent. At the end of the day, we have little control over the thoughts and motivations of those who surround us. But even in the worst of situations; even when you find yourself in the midst of circumstances that suggest your intelligence, your education, your ambition, your drive are each factors relegated to a space of irrelevancy, how you react to those perceptions are completely within your power and under your personal control. With that in mind, you must commit to yourself to be unwavering in your determination not to give others the power to define your future, limit your vision, or in any way, set parameters on what you know to be the full breadth of your personal possibilities.

You might wonder, with so much stacked against me, why even try? The odds, it seems, are so overwhelmingly unforgiving, why even invest the time in a journey that is likely to end in defeat? Why even begin a quest toward leadership when the chance of success seems so dismally remote? To that perspective, I pose the following question. At what point have the odds ever been in our favor? At what precise moment did we, as Black women, have the wind at our backs, pushing, lifting, carrying us along, and effortlessly guiding us in the direction of our dreams? The truth of the matter is, we've always carried a heavier burden. But it's never stopped us before, and neither should it now.

It is true, however, that the reality of our circumstances is indeed difficult to face. Stated simply, it hurts. But as we learned previously, it makes no sense to try to deny this pain, run away from it, or attempt to bury it somewhere deep inside our personal psyche, never to be retrieved again. Instead, we must summon the courage to draw upon it, and then use it to push us in the direction of our greatest possibilities. As Zora Neal Hurston keenly observed, "If you're silent about your pain, they'll kill you, and say you enjoyed it." Now is the time to stop being silent. Now is the time to be loud, bold, and purposeful in fighting for the advancement of Black women specifically, instead of merely pushing in support of increased women's representation in the abstract. As we've seen here, seeking the advancement of women generally, all too often results in leaving Black women behind specifically. At best, we find ourselves little more than crumbs at the table of gendered inclusion. It's time to be a key component of the main course.

> "Seeking the advancement of women generally, all too often results in leaving Black women behind specifically."

As we begin this work, and move unapologetically on behalf of our own full and fair share of leadership inclusion, we do so knowing that our efforts will help ensure that the rich diversity of this nation will be more fully reflected across the spectrum of decision-makers within institutions of power. We do so knowing that we can't afford to merely wait our turn. We do so understanding that we can no longer stand quietly aside while others leave us further and further behind. Sistahs, we must face the harsh reality that it won't just happen on its own. Instead, we must strategize together, learn from one another, lean on each other, and when necessary, fight for one another.

Now to be sure, we needn't do everything by ourselves. There are those who are ready and willing to help. But rest assured, if we don't prioritize our own advancement, no one else will either. In the end, it's up to us to move beyond merely requesting some larger piece of an ever-shrinking pie, but instead, to change the very ingredients with which it's primarily comprised.

With that imperative in mind, we must bravely face the cold reality that as it stands today, we are nearly non-existent as corporate leaders, severely under-represented as non-profit leaders, dangerously under-resourced as entrepreneurs, and largely confined to a narrow subset of opportunities within the public sphere. Undoubtedly, all of this is true. But the same was true for United States Congresswoman Gwen Moore, Member of the U. S. House of Representatives, and the first Black person of either gender to win election to Congress from the state of Wisconsin.[49] I seem to believe the same can be said about Mayor Stephanie Rawlings-Blake, one of only three Black women in the nation to serve as Mayor of a top 100 city, or Sharene Wood, President and CEO of 5001 Flavors, Owner of Harlem

Haberdashery, and designer to the stars. Natalie CoField, CEO of the Greater Austin Black Chamber of Commerce and Founder of the powerhouse non-profit, Walker's Legacy might also know a little about this harsh reality; as might Charisse Lillie, President of the Comcast Foundation, along with Denise Evans, Vice President of Market Development for IBM, or Shellye Archambeau, CEO of MetricStream. Perhaps Ambassador Suzan Johnson Cook, former U.S. Ambassador-at-Large for Religious Freedom, or even Bishop Carlotta Vaughn of Preachers of Detroit could relate, as could Vanessa De Luca, Editor-in-Chief of Essence Magazine.

Now ask yourself, what is the difference between you and each of these amazing women? Do they have a special genetic composition that makes them impervious to discrimination? Was their brilliance so overwhelmingly obvious that no one dared stand in their way? Were they born under the protection of good fortune, finding luck on their side at each turn upon life's journey? Not in the least. You will learn in the chapters that follow that none of these things are true. Perhaps only one significant difference between your situation and theirs exists. Unlike you, none of them had the benefit of their very own community of women who gathered together for one specific purpose—to generously give of their wisdom with the expressed intent of providing guidance along their professional journey. They made mistakes. At times, they stumbled. But ultimately, they each made it to the top. Now, through their generosity and that of many others, so will you.

"What if you allowed yourself the luxury of the notion that it is your knowledge, your instincts, your capabilities, and yes, your leadership that is precisely needed for such a time as this?"

Before you press on, take a brief respite to prepare yourself for all that is yet to unfold. Imagine, for a moment, what could be possible if you became personally invested in shifting the dynamic under which you gauge your possibilities. What if you came to the unwavering decision to discontinue any complicit acceptance of things as they are, and instead, allowed yourself the freedom to shape the future in the image in which you perceive it should be? What if you accepted that it is both within your power and your responsibility to define the dynamics of normalcy such that it will bend in the direction of the coming increasingly diverse world? What if you allowed yourself the luxury of the notion that it is your knowledge, your instincts, your capabilities, and yes, your leadership that is precisely needed for such a time as this? What if you simply made up your mind that no matter the obstacle, and despite the obstructionist, nothing and no one will stand in your way?

Let not the odds be your guide as to your possibilities in life. Make your own odds. Take off the shackles of pre-defined limitations, and fully and freely, allow yourself to soar.

Exceptional Black Woman Vision & Action Guide

1. What is your biggest & boldest leadership ambition?

2. Where are you now along that journey? Where would you like to be one year from now, five years from now, a decade in the future?

3. Are you ready to commit to the daily actions necessary to make your way to the top?

If you now find yourself feeling isolated along your leadership journey, know that you are not alone. The facts relayed throughout this chapter provide some context to your personal experience. In the pages that follow, you will gain a greater understanding of the specific challenges you will face along with perspectives and proven techniques utilized by those who have successfully navigated the journey upon which you have chosen to embark. Learn these lessons well. And know that as they made it to the top, so can you!

CHAPTER 2

What You're Up Against

> **❝** *The road ahead is not going to be easy. It never is, especially for folks like you and me. Because while we've come so far, the truth is those age-old problems are stubborn, and they haven't fully gone away.* **❞**

—Michelle Obama
First Lady of the United States
Addressing the 2015 Graduating Class of Tuskegee University

When Michelle Obama stood before the 2015 graduating class of Tuskegee University, few could have predicted that her message would relay with blatant honesty the specific challenges she has faced and continues to face, even as First Lady of the United States, with the intersecting experience of being a Black woman in America. She reminded the graduates of how a celebratory fist-bump between herself and her husband was somehow widely characterized in a major media outlet as a "terrorist fist jab." And she recalled how some commentators had once described her as exhibiting "a little bit of uppity-ism," while another had referred to her as "Obama's Baby Mama." But beyond reflecting on her own experiences, she took great pains to warn the graduates of the world that awaits, a world that is still deeply immersed in the realities of race.[50]

"The world won't always see you in those caps and gowns. They won't know how hard you worked and how much you sacrificed to make it to this day—the countless hours you spent studying to

get this diploma, the multiple jobs you worked to pay for school, the times you had to drive home and take care of your grandma, the evenings you gave up to volunteer at a food bank or organize a campus fundraiser, they don't know that part of you.

Instead, they will make assumptions about who they think you are based on their limited notion of the world. And my husband and I know how frustrating that experience can be. We've both felt the sting of those daily slights throughout our entire lives—the folks who crossed the street in fear of their safety; the clerks who kept a close eye on us in all those department stores; the people at formal events who assumed we were the "help"— and those who have questioned our intelligence, our honesty, even our love of this country.

And I know that these indignities are obviously nothing compared to what folks across the country are dealing with every single day — those nagging worries that you're going to get stopped or pulled over for absolutely no reason; the fear that your job application will be overlooked because of the way your name sounds; the agony of sending your kids to schools that may not be separate, but are far from equal; the realization that no matter how far you rise in life, how hard you work to be a good person, a good parent, a good citizen — for some folks, it will never be enough.[51]"

With eloquence and honesty, the First Lady succinctly encapsulated not only the realities faced by the President and herself but the overriding truth of what it really means to be Black in America. Here's the truth—*if achieving were as simple as merely being the best, you might have already reached your boldest and biggest career aspirations.* But the real world is much more complicated than that, is it not? The real world is one in which human beings either consciously or unconsciously attach significance to difference. In this way, we link traits, perceptions, and anticipated possibility to entire groups of humanity. Over time, this

"If achieving were as simple as merely being the best, you might have already reached your boldest aspirations."

deeply ingrained tradition results in the development of a complex web of advantages and disadvantages reflexively provided to individuals based on where they stand along the human continuum of valued vs. devalued status. The differing realities that come about as a result, can be stark, or they can be subtle. They can be blatant, or they can be hard to exactly pinpoint. Nevertheless, they exist. Over time, this dual reality, or mirrored fate provided to individuals based on cultural valuations becomes normalized, and seen as *"just the way things are"* or *"have always been"*, or to some, the way they're *"supposed to be."*

To be a Black woman is to exist in a constant state of navigation. Forever negotiating invisible pitfalls and challenges that others too often fail to see, or even acknowledge exist at all. To succeed at exceptional levels, you must become a master navigator. In facing the dual challenges of both race and gender in a cultural context that privileges all that you are not, you must learn how to overcome both external and internal challenges that can handicap your ability to fully and freely actualize your greatest potential.

Clearly, when even the First Lady of the United States finds it impossible to escape fully the implications of overriding cultural realities that still castigates her Blackness along with her womanhood, it highlights the degree to which these challenges remain real for us all. But it's important to keep in mind that it's not necessary to fully abolish this reality to achieve within it. Certainly, the endgoal must be to ultimately create a society where all are empowered with boundless opportunity based on personal ability and drive to achieve. But of course, you can't afford to wait for that ideal day.

You must begin now, in earnest, the pursuit of your biggest and boldest ambitions. And you must begin knowing that your special task entails learning how to achieve despite the distinct pitfalls you will face, the unfair nature of the battlefield, and the unearned advantages others will be extended and will be able to exploit. This is a challenge you must commit to mastering if you will one day win. Individual victories in the midst of institutionalized unfairness is an absolute necessity. It's a requirement to not only get you where you *deserve* to be, but when replicated over and over again, it's also necessary to one day amass enough collective power so as to ultimately bring unfair formal and information institutions tumbling to the ground. Know that your success is not a trivial matter. Your exercised potential will lay the groundwork for a better future for us all.

Conquering the Battle Within

Navigating the challenge of race, is a battle that must be waged as both an external *and* internal process, particularly when racial subjugation is linked to a history of violent oppression. Psychologists and neuroscientists have each found that psychological and biological implications of traumatic experiences can, in fact, linger for generations. This phenomenon is known as "intergenerational trauma." Such trauma is said to derive from violence-laden acts which, in essence, produce such a strong imprint on individuals who experience it firsthand that implications span generations beyond those specific individuals whom originally suffered the traumatic ordeal. For example, *descendants* of the Holocaust and 9/11 survivors have each been found to be three times more likely to be diagnosed with Post-Traumatic Stress Disorder (PTSD) than similar children descendant from those who did not undergo those traumatic experiences.[52]

Likewise, Native American children descendent of a legacy of brutality that dates back for centuries, have been found to exhibit similar indicators resulting in personality features such as "numbness, sadness, inhibition, anxiety, hyper-vigilance, and a not-unreasonable sense that the outside world [is] implacably hostile."[53]

The African American experience, of course, is one that was birthed in trauma. It is a history that began with the brutality of the Trans-Atlantic Slave Trade, the largest forced deportation of human beings in the entire history of this planet. This global enterprise lasted for nearly four centuries and resulted in the ripping of millions of Africans from their homeland, and in the process, left millions at the bottom of the ocean.[54] For those who survived the brutal deportation experience, the new reality that faced them on the other side of their journey was no less horrific. As practiced in the United States, the institution of slavery was not only a life-long sentence, but it was also passed down maternally. Hence, since enslaved Africans were interpreted as "property" slave-owners could increase their asset holdings specifically through the sexual violation of Black women. The result was a new, horrifying reality for Africans who were forced into a lifetime of unpaid labor, and an institution that was enforced through the systemization of unspeakable brutality, along with the ever-presence of rape, murder and the commonplace occurrence of ripping apart families so as to maintain compliance and maximize economic outcomes.

Hilary Beard, entrepreneur, best-selling author, and former corporate executive believes that the implications of this experience remain with us and in fact, may manifest as inhibitors to our current success. She explains,

> *"Fear became encoded in our DNA. We are people who were systematically and intentionally terrorized by white people in this country. The intention of that terror was to keep us in our place, and our place was serving them—being exploited and being exploitable. And so, that's encoded in our DNA. I think it's important to understand that we're not in those times. Even though we might have reactions—primal reactions because our brains and bodies have been wired to protect us because of our ancestral experience. But that's not the world we live in right now. So there are ways we need to challenge ourselves. Use counseling, use community, to come together and overcome."*

Portland State University Professor, Joy Leary, takes this perspective a step further. She posits that while the systematic dehumanization of enslaved Africans was the initial trauma, successive generations have continued to experience trauma based upon a racial hierarchy within which popular culture provides advantages and disadvantages based on skin color that dramatically affects the likelihood of success. This experience, which she describes as Post-Traumatic Slave Syndrome, can negatively impact African American self-perception leading to, among other things, feelings of self-doubt, rebelliousness, hopelessness, or an overall questioning of self-worth.[55]

What is also true, and at least worth acknowledgement here, is the fact that as it relates to professional achievement we operate each and every day within a cultural context that only relatively recently, allowed us admittance onto a field of opportunity ostensibly unregulated by caste-like structures within which we are forbidden to cross. And so we find ourselves today, descended from the survivors of 250 years of a particularly brutal slave experience, established and maintained through the constant threat and application of violence. We're also the children of those who endured roughly an additional century of continuous indignities and random terror that was institutionalized through the application of the Black Codes and followed swiftly by Jim Crow. So while we now find ourselves 150 years beyond the American slave experience, we are still relative newcomers to freedom. If we were to take the 1964 and 1965 Civil Rights and Voting Rights Acts as the starting point of lasting, litigious freedom in America, that would mean that after having lived and labored within this nation for more than 400 years, we've only had the ability to experience lasting, albeit begrudging freedom for 50 of those years. In short, the overwhelming majority of our experience in America is one that has been laced in a tragic interplay of both economic exploitation and consistent exposure to violence-based trauma. Those experiences are not simply washed away with time. They leave scars. It is this reality that you must be willing to face boldly and acknowledge to be able to move forward with confidence and in self-love.

Understand that your distinct legacy is not one of victimization, it is one of strength and survival. You are descendant from the strongest of the strong. Those who exhibited the courage, wit, and strength to face one of the most brutal crimes against humanity to ever occur on this planet, and ultimately survive. Only with this understanding of who you are and from whence you came firmly in place, will you be

> "Understand that your distinct legacy is not one of victimization, it is one of strength and survival."

properly equipped to fight the battles that most assuredly lie ahead. You are the fruit of those who faced the worst aspects of humankind and still had the audacity to live.

Facing and Overcoming a Legacy of Trauma

The most important questions raised by all of this is how are we to finally rid ourselves of the baggage of a traumatic past, especially when that baggage may occur reflexively as a result of our biological heritage rather than through the process of logical thought? Likewise, how do we escape modern-day disturbing occurrences specific to the Black experience generally, and to the experiences of Black women specifically? How do we overcome the psychological residue of trauma, either past or present, without allowing it to unconsciously and consistently seep into our psyche, and ultimately impact every aspect of our personal and professional lives?

Most experts agree, to overcome the impact of collective trauma and move forward constructively, traumatic occurrences must be faced. There is healing in truth. And at a minimum, truth requires the acknowledgment of past transgressions. That's why massive atrocities are often responded to within the world community with calls for international tribunals, reparations, or as in the South African experience, the establishment of a Truth and Reconciliation Commission. Acknowledgment and remembrance are powerful. It is a

> "There is healing in truth."

tradition that is, for example, well woven into Jewish culture. Deeply embedded within Jewish traditions is the practice of regular acknowledgment and reverence for the ability to endure unspeakable atrocities and still, as a people, survive. These traditions go as far as to include an annual holy day, Yom Ha-Shoah, specifically dedicated to the memory of the Holocaust. Such practices are seemingly in-line with the most commonly utilized treatment for PTSD, Cognitive Behavioral Therapy (CBT). The entire goal of CBT is the reprocessing of memories until they are crafted into a narrative that no longer has its sting.[56]

The challenge with the African American experience is that unlike the Holocaust, American-implemented traumas, especially related to the Black experience, are rarely acknowledged or if brought up at all, are quickly mini-

> "You exist within a broader culture that in many ways refuse to affirm your reality."

mized. In fact, our national aversion to honest exchanges around race runs so deep, that the subject's mere mention is often cast itself, as racially offensive. As such, racism—either past or present—has quickly devolved to "that which shall not be named" status in America. The prevailing position espoused by many of those within the dominant culture is typically one of two defensive retorts. On one hand, there is a common assertion that every traumatic experience that was wreaked upon African Americans before, up to, and including the Civil Rights Movement, are historical in nature, and therefore, completely irrelevant to contemporary reality and unnecessary to revisit in any substantive way. However, when evidence of contemporary individual acts or institutionalized racism is revealed, the common reaction is a suspension of belief. The prevailing and often espoused retort in those situations are, "If I haven't experienced it, then it must not be happening to you." Or if by chance, some misfortune has befallen you, it must be because of a personal deficiency or because you did something to deserve it.[57]

Be aware that it is possible that continual dismissals of contemporary and past racist transgressions can lead to overwhelming feelings of self-doubt. If you're not careful, it can cause you to question your own value, your own capabilities and your own sense of belonging. It can cut off from the root, the very sense of confidence and efficacy that is absolutely essential for leadership success.

Know this. You exist within a broader culture that in many ways refuse to affirm your reality. This does not make your experiences any less *real*. It does not serve as an indicator of your brilliance or a reflection of your value. Instead, it denotes a culture that prefers a state of mass denial, rather than live up to the responsibility of truth. It chooses this course because any acknowledgment of truth based on a foundation of morality would require corrective action. And in a hyper-competitive zero-sum and highly materialistic culture, corrective action would result in a reduction of opportunities for those who have for centuries enjoyed advantages, some invisible and others in plain emboldened view. One need only to examine the contemporary political dynamics surrounding any discussion of reparations for those descended from the American slave experience or the continuing controversy around affirmative action to see that America openly rejects this moral imperative. It instead prefers to operate under the illusion of "color blindness" and an openly espoused but yet to be realized state of equality of opportunity.

Know that this is the field of play you have inherited. Is it fair? No. Can it be changed? Perhaps. But in the interim, you must learn how to navigate and operate successfully within it, without losing your faith in you. Will your path to leadership be as direct and unencumbered as those who are not forced to traverse this much more challenging and potentially personally deprecating route? Probably not. But that doesn't mean you can't get there. That doesn't mean, you can't win.

Uncovering the Existence and Persistence of Unconscious Bias

Professional spaces are of course, beyond the days of socially acceptable overt racism. Still, one of the biggest challenges that persists is the continued presence of biases that dwell just below the surface and deep within the subconscious mind. In other words, your challenge is not only to master a cultural context that continues to perpetuate systems of advantage and disadvantage that are so hard-wired as to be institutional in nature, you must also overcome individual biases that science has now found to be nothing short of reflexively projected by the human brain.

Since the 1980s, neuroscientists and psychologists have conducted dozens of studies which have each established the existence of unconscious bias. This body of work has found that in various contexts, even those who openly reject the idea of discrimination, and fail to see themselves as prejudiced, in practice, often engage in discriminatory behavior. The predisposition to perceive or treat people differently based on race is pervasive, and can pop up in the most unexpected circumstances. Even doctors, who've taken an oath to at the very least, do no harm, are not exempt from this tendency. Several studies have shown that Black and White patients are treated differently. Black patients, for example, are less likely to be provided pain medication [58] and more likely to experience delays in medical treatment.[59] In some cases, Blacks fail to be treat altogether, even when exhibiting symptoms of potentially deadly illnesses.[60] Certainly, if bias shows up in these high-stakes, life or death situations, it's relatively easy to understand how it can be nothing short of commonplace at work.

Often deeply implanted in organizational culture, bias can manifest itself in numerous ways. In the hiring process, for example, MIT and the University of Chicago found that resumes reflecting average qualifications and associated with White-sounding names are actually more likely to receive a callback than resumes reflecting high qualifications that are associated with Black-sounding names.[61] It's also been well-established that gender-bias significantly diminishes hiring prospects for women in male-dominated occupations.[62]

But beyond the hiring process, bias lives and breathes within the work environment itself, most notably through daily micro-affirmations—the consistent opening of doors of opportunity, gestures of inclusion, or the provision of comfort, support, and insider-information to one specific group and not others.[63] The implications of this can mean that opportunities for promotions or other professional advancements are more readily available to the specific demographic group that reflects organizational norms around who is *perceived* to be an achiever. These perceptions are typically driven by the organization's present and previous leadership and often drive notions around who is and who is not a good "fit" for the organization. Such a reality can cause discriminatory outcomes to become self-perpetuating in nature. And as to the specific circumstances of Black women, research suggests that bias ultimately causes Black women to be ignored altogether, as "Black executives" are consistently perceived as men, where "female executives" are typically thought of as White women.[64]

While it's impossible to know with complete certainty if any of the circumstances described here occur as a result of unconscious bias, explicit racism, sexism, or some combination of each of these factors, the fact remains that the playing field is clearly not a level one. The biggest challenge in combating this reality will not merely require a change in cultural dynamics dating back centuries; it also requires overriding the natural, reflexive wiring of the human brain.

The Science of Discrimination

Neuroscientists have found that our brains are made up of primarily three different areas which each have very different functions. The neocortex, the limbic brain, and what's commonly referred to as the reptilian brain. Each area operates independently of one another and serves different functions. The neocortex controls language, abstract thought, and imagination. And because of its flexibility, it is believed that this portion of the brain has almost infinite learning abilities. In contrast, the reptilian brain controls our vital functions—the heart, breathing, our body temperature and balance. It's rigid, regulated, and reliable in its function. But the limbic brain is quite distinct from the other two regions. Detached from logical thought and control of vital bodily function, its role is centered on human emotion, and among other things, is home to the amygdala, an almond-shaped wad of neurons that unconsciously reacts to fear and threat. Reflexive rather than reasoned, it is this specific portion of the brain that scientists have found to be correlated to implicit racial bias.[65] [66]

Let's face it. In modern society, we're bombarded by information. Much more, in fact, than our brains are even capable of processing in any logical way. It's estimated that in the course of our daily lives, we receive 11 million bits of information per second. [67] Yet our brains can only consciously process a maximum of 60 bits per second.[68] That means about 99.999994% of all the information we receive is actually processed by our subconscious mind. Our brains use shortcuts to instantaneously make sense of the world around us at any given moment. With this all too human tendency applied in a cultural context that is rife with stereotypical notions around race, gender, sexual orientation, and any number of points of difference, it makes sense that reflexive reactions are actually based on prevailing stereotypes[69] rather than the more time-consuming process of logical thought, influenced by evidence associated with each individual or situation to be assessed. In short, our brains are simply wired to take shortcuts. And within an environment that is literally polluted by centuries of oppressively negative associations related to African Americans, and layered with patriarchal assumptions around the "place" of women in society at-large, the result is a reality that both normalizes and compounds bias in virtually every aspect of Black women's lives.

Facing Unfairness

Given this reality, how do you win? How do you overcome unfairness that is literally baked into the human psyche? How do you fight back against organizations that have institutionalized (knowingly or not) a culture of unfairness? The truth of the matter is that the responsibility for effectively addressing this problem is two-fold. Organizations need to acknowledge overtly the reality of both unconscious bias and micro-affirmations at work and invest in aggressive staff training that provides not only an understanding of these factors but also provide strategies that help decision-makers overcome these all-too-human inclinations. It's this part of the equation that's an important sliver of what my company does in an attempt to combat this problem at the source. This is a point that cannot be glazed over. Organizations have a responsibility to actively fight unconscious bias in their own backyard. Not just because it's the right thing to do, but because it's the fiscally sound thing to do, especially as it relates to positioning themselves to attract and retain talent that will allow them to gain a competitive edge in an increasingly diverse marketplace.

But the fact of the matter is, institutional change takes time. Especially changes that require humans to quite literally retrain their brains. And so, as important as working at the source of the problem is, it's not

"Your ability to control others is limited at best. But the ability to control yourself is absolute."

enough. Quite simply, you can't afford to wait for every company to recognize the critical nature of this problem and then seek to train their way out of it. The best way to take control of your own future in every aspect of life is to take responsibility for it yourself. Your ability to control others is limited at best. But the ability to control yourself is absolute. You must embrace the role of becoming the master of your own destiny. You must be willing to find a way to the success that you seek. But you needn't search blindly for those strategies which provide the highest likelihood of getting you where you want to go and where you know you belong. You're in the right place. It's precisely this guidance the subsequent chapters will meticulously unfold.

Exceptional Black Women Vision & Action Guide

1. Your destiny is not one of victimization. It is one of strength and survival. Take a moment to reflect on someone in your family tree, past or present, who epitomizes this sentiment. What challenges did they overcome in their lives? What aspects of their strength and tenacity do you see reflected in you? How does that make you feel about your ability to face and overcome the modern-day hurdles you face?

2. Take a moment to reflect on an experience that you believe you were subjected to merely because of your race or gender. What happened? How did it make you feel? Know that your disappointment, sadness, or even anger associated with that experience is legitimate. You have a right to your emotions. And you have the strength to carry on.

3. Being on the receiving end of racism and/or sexism hurts. It's draining—mentally, physically, and spiritually. If you're not careful, it will chip away at the best parts of who you are now and everything you were meant to be. To deal with the elevated stress that is endemic with the Black woman's experience, you must commit to carving out special time for yourself on a daily basis. Whether that time consists of meditation, prayer, exercise, or all of the above, you must allow yourself a moment to decompress, reflect, and renew. Consider this your daily non-negotiable act of self-love. What daily action will you commit to now to fill this need in your life?

PART II
This is How You Win

CHAPTER 3

Free. Your. Mind.

❝ *I want women to know they are empowered. I want women to know that whatever it is they conceive in their mind, can be done. With the right people, with the right resources, and the right relationships, all things are possible. I want fear not to stop us, but to inspire us to be the best we can be.* **❞**

—Toya Powell
Founder, Bid Compliance Solutions

I have the honor of working with absolutely brilliant women. At the beginning of our coaching relationship, many of these women seemingly have no idea of the extent of their giftedness. Instead, they've allowed self-doubt, hostile work environments, external unconstructive criticism, or just plain professional isolation, to create a perfect storm of doubt within which they've dwelled for years. Still, they have dreams. Achievable dreams. Dreams that are well within their expertise and professional capabilities. But by the time they come to me, it becomes immediately clear what's responsible for their inability to break through.

The problem isn't a lack of skills, an unsavory work ethic, or even in some cases, a dearth of critically important connections—a key factor that keeps many equally brilliant women partitioned away from the success they seek. For these women, even with so many advantages that others would envy, somehow, for years, they found themselves locked within a self-imposed prison of fear. As a result, they moved through their careers operating at only a fraction of their full capabilities. So they stayed stuck, somewhere deep below their stated ambitions and clear potential. They stayed inhibited because somewhere deep inside of them, their fear had them convinced, that they needn't even try.

Escaping the Prison of Fear

There is perhaps no bigger inhibitor to achieving exceptional levels of success than the barrier of fear. Fear of the unknown. Fear of other people's judgments. Fear of failure. And for some, even fear of success. Fear, is the great inhibitor. It has the power to keep you forever locked within the boundaries of mediocracy. It has the power to keep you forever isolated from your dream.

Of course, no one is impervious to this all-too-human emotion, and neither should you be. Like pain, fear has a clear and critical purpose. For most of human history, fear has served as our protector. It alerts us to the presence of potential danger, and thus, is a critical survival mechanism. Even to this day, in certain dire circumstances, I'm sure, fear saves lives.

But in the professional context, fear kills dreams. It will keep you stuck in the sanctuary of the familiar and secluded from your greatest potential. To reach your biggest and boldest leadership ambitions, you either learn to master fear or fear will become your master.

Of course, as is the case with all human emotion, fear will never, nor should it ever be completely eliminated. The trick is not just to control it, but instead, redirect it. Become in tune to your fear, and those factors that have spawned it and instead of seeking to dismiss it completely, begin to interpret that same sensation from an entirely different perspective. Know that within the workplace environment, you must consciously detach yourself from the natural tendency to perceive fear as your protector. Instead, interpret it as a motivator. Know that it's there to alert you that the stakes are high, or that the road is unfamiliar, or that others doubt your ability to execute or perform at high levels. Yes, each of these scenarios and more are high-stakes situations, but they are not dangerous. You will survive. You will learn. And eventually, you will thrive. Use the fear you feel deep inside as fuel to motivate you to prepare with more gusto and then perform at your best, always knowing that each experience will result in lessons learned. Overtime, the accumulation of experiences will eventually lead to greater confidence, which then will lead to a reduction in fear, and ultimately, improved outcomes.

Understanding and Acquiring the Mindset of a Leader

Even with the challenge of fear largely behind you, know that you will never fully develop into a leader until you first obtain the *mind* of a leader. Simply put, leaders *think* differently. They believe bigger. They try harder. And they see opportunity where others see only difficulty, failure, or defeat. Within them resides a sense of quiet confidence that no matter the challenge, they have what it takes to not only face it, but they also have what it takes to rally the troops and win.

Even beyond these core traits, the Black women leaders I spent over two years interviewing each shared certain commonalities that are most certainly directly responsible for their exceptional levels of success, even under the most difficult of circumstances. These women are not only confident, but they're also resilient. They're not only knowledgeable and exceedingly skilled, but they also believe in continual improvement. In other words, they're not shy about expanding their skill-set over and over again. This habit allowed them the ability to grow into opportunities as they appeared. And ultimately, their sense of self-efficacy in many instances actually *created* opportunities where none had previously existed. To a person, they believed in and exhibited a strong work ethic. And finally, they each had an external grounding. A foundation of strength that was forged in family, faith, or a sense of responsibility to something bigger than themselves as evidenced by love of community and in many cases, a personal imperative to impact change.

51

Where There is Vision, There is Success

Who is Angie LeMar? She is *only* the top Black woman comedienne in all of Great Britain. A born performer, she admittedly caught the bug at an early age, but like many in her field, her comedic chops were initially developed as a defensive mechanism. Having struggled with severe dyslexia as a child, Angie would craft jokes on the fly to deflect the task of reading in front of her class. But even with this severe disability, she always believed in herself. She always knew, "I can do this."

So brick by brick, she built a career as a stand-up comedienne and quickly became a hot commodity. She reflects, "Everybody wanted to book me. Everyone wanted me on their [play]bill." Eventually, she was offered a documentary that would showcase her segue to the American comedic platform. And so a film crew followed her as she came across the pond to play the Apollo and audition for the then, top-rated Cosby Show. After filming was done, word came back to her that the producers decided not to go through with the project. They believed the film couldn't work because it was too positive. "There was no downside," they complained.

> "You have to get on your dream track."

It was at this critical juncture in her career that Angie learned an invaluable lesson that ultimately allowed her to forge a new path and accelerate her success to previously unforeseen heights. She remembers thinking to herself distinctly, "You will never do that to me again." She understood that when you leave your fate completely in the hands of others, they can pull the rug out from under you at any time. And when word gets out of the perceived failure, the impacts on your career could be devastating. So instead of merely shrinking away from that disappointment, she regrouped; and took the time to reimagine a future that put her in greater control of her own destiny.

To become the master of her own fate, Angie understood that she had to develop an entirely new skill. So she started writing her own material, not only stand-ups, but entire theatrical performances. And before long, her career was bigger and better than it had ever been. The lesson she learned along the way was that ultimately, your career, your future, your life, is in your own hands. You must be willing to live up to the responsibility to literally create the future of your dreams. And sometimes that means you must be willing to grow in new areas and learn new things, to be able to do what you've never done, go where you've never been, and breakthrough to an entirely new level of success.

"You just have to get on your dream track and be very clear. I knew from a very young age that I wanted to make people laugh. And that's all that I wanted to do. I was gifted to do this. And the fact that I was Black, that I was fat, the fact that I had all these things against me, wasn't going to get in my way."

What's beautiful about Angie's path is that she was very resolute in her *decision* to succeed. Even as a child, she had a vision for the future she wanted to create for herself, and she resolved to not let anything get in her way. And so even when she faced set backs along the way, she wasn't discouraged. If anything, she became even more focused on her vision and more determined to figure out how to best bring it to fruition. For her, it's not just that failure wasn't an option, it's more like failure was not even a part of the equation. Her entire focus wasn't on whether or not she would succeed, it was on figuring out *how* to get there, and then doing what was necessary to not only stay there but to engage in the continuous process of moving to the next level of success.

"One thing I know for sure for myself is that the dream is a private dream. And it's a really honest dream when you say, of course, I can do this. I trust myself. I believe in myself. And it might not be the timing that everyone else does it. It might be the stuff that [you] do later on in life, but everything you do right now should take you toward that dream. Don't go off track and make a mess of your life."

Though Angie now lives much of her life within the spotlight, her deepest strengths, those most responsible for her amazing career success, took shape far away from center stage. It's in this space, what she terms "her private zone" that the mindset of a leader, the mindset of a winner, comes fully into view.

"When I'm in my private zone, I'm the best. I am the most beautiful. I am amazing. Even when I was young, I would come out of my room, and in my mind, the paparazzi was waiting outside, and I'd come out the room saying, 'Not now. Can you leave me alone?' I was doing interviews in my room, saying, 'I can't talk about that right now, that's my personal life, I just don't know.' I was collecting awards, and I was holding awards, and I was saying, 'There are so many people I would like to thank right now.' And I had it all in my heart. It was part of my little ritual. Because if I never won an award, I'd already won an award. I'd given it to myself. But I had that determination that said, I'm going to get it. My belief in myself was so strong that I knew I was going to be amazing."

"What I want to say to every woman is to stay in your lane, your dream lane. Don't watch anybody else. Because they'll always be someone more attractive than you, they'll always be skinnier than you, they'll always be lighter, darker, everything that we put on ourselves that slows us down. I visualize things from a very deep place, and I just walk towards what I visualize. Protect your vision. It's your thoughts. It's your plan. It's your story. Just make sure that you use it!"

Angie's strong sense of vision and faith in her ability to transfer vision to reality has been a constant in her life, and a gift she's drawn upon time and time again to excel, even within the ultra-competitive and sometimes fickle world that is show-business. She has, at the end of the day, been the leader of her own destiny, and it's within this space that she continues to shine.

Confidence and Courageousness

Entrepreneur and former corporate executive, LaFern Batie comes by her boldness honestly. As the youngest of six, she's always had to speak up to be heard. Now the leader of her own successful consulting firm, LaFern has a clear understanding of what confidence is, and what it is not. "Confidence," she says, "is not perfection. But it's knowing that everything you need is accessible. It's knowing that what you're created to be

> "Confidence is not perfection. It's knowing that everything you need is accessible."

is enough. It's refusing to be paralyzed by perfection. It's being willing to fail and learn from those failures, and then getting up and asking yourself, what did I learn? And committing not to make those same mistakes again."

What's critical about LaFern's perspective is that her confidence is not static. It is in fact, confidence in motion. It's the willingness to act, to potentially fail, to learn from those failures, recalibrate, and try again.

Like LaFern, Dr. Dorothy Buckhanan Wilson, International President of Alpha Kappa Alpha Sorority, Inc. and Sr. Vice President of Goodwill Industries parlayed confidence and competence into extraordinary success in multiple spaces; as a corporate leader, as a non-profit leader, and as the leader of a major international service organization. For her, multidimensional success was all but inevitable due to her unwavering belief in herself, a stellar work-ethic, a willingness to take risks, and when necessary, the courage to start over from square one.

From Dorothy's perspective, she never doubted her ability to out-smart or out-work anyone. As she succinctly puts it, "That's how I was raised." Interestingly, part of this unwavering confidence spawned directly from a crystal clear, but no doubt painful memory that provided for her, inspiration, and most likely, a sense of responsibility to succeed.

> *"I remember going to the voting polls with my grandfather. He was asked to count the jelly beans in the jar. I was there as a small child, holding my grandfather's hand when he wasn't allowed to vote. The blood, the tears, everything, was shed for that very basic right. He knew that educating his grandchildren was going to be the way. When my grandfather sent me off to college, he changed the whole trajectory of our family."*

With this humble beginning, this small-town South Carolina girl went on to receive dual undergraduate degrees in Economics and Business and ultimately earned her MBA before building a successful corporate career in Marketing and Brand Management. Her willingness to face the unknown and believe in her ability to master new challenges and soar was a central component of her stellar success.

"I was willing to take risks. I was willing to relocate. I was willing to change careers. I felt that if it was an opportunity that made sense, I would figure out how to make it work."

Dorothy's willingness to "figure it out" is an essential indicator of what Psychologist, Carol Dweck calls, a "growth mindset." Her research has found that essentially, people tend to exhibit two types of perspectives on the world. Those who exhibit a "fixed mindset," or who hold the belief that your talents, abilities, and intelligence is a fixed quality, and those who have a "growth mindset," or have the basic belief that through hard work and persistence, they can literally grow their skill set to meet a particular challenge or need.

People who exhibit a fixed mindset, in essence, believe they either have it—talent, skill, intelligence—or they don't. So when faced with a challenging situation they tend to shut down and in most instances either quickly quit difficult tasks or fail to even try due to the belief that if something doesn't come easily to them, then it must be because it lies beyond their capabilities. Their natural inclination is to avoid the frustration or potential embarrassment of engaging in a difficult task, and so more often than not, they fail to even try. From their perspective, any effort would be a wasted effort because they have predetermined the task at hand to be beyond their capabilities. Fixed-mindset individuals, in essence, *live* within their comfort zone. They do what comes easy. They perform only in areas in which they know from the start; they can master, or, at least, avoid criticism. In their element, they can be nothing short of genius. But ask them to move one inch beyond, and they fall apart.

The tragedy that's inherent with this perspective on life is that it preordains a consistent state of underperformance. Research shows that it's possible to literally grow and strengthen your brain at any age. Each time you learn something new or practice a skill over and over again, you are actually strengthening a network of neurons. Over time, these connections become thick, literally linking brain cells. As a result, stimulating one neuron in the sequence, now more easily triggers the next one to fire. And the more times this network is stimulated, the stronger and more efficient it becomes. As you engage in the practice of challenging yourself, over time those things you once found to be difficult, or possibly even impossible to master, eventually become easy to you. It is literally through this process of consistently pushing your boundaries, and exerting the necessary effort to practice and learn something new that your brain physically and literally becomes stronger and smarter.

Stellar performers like Dorothy, LaFern, and frankly, all of the women included in this book, seemed to instinctively understand that their natural abilities were just the beginning of their greatness. They met the challenge of unfamiliar opportunities with increased gusto, focus, and a willingness to put in the work that's necessary to learn, even by trial and error if that's what it took, until they became a master in an entirely new realm. Their "growth mindset," or belief in their ability to lean into new challenges and come out the other side as holders of an entirely new area of mastery is not only a key component to successful leadership; it's absolutely essential for ever-increasing success in life.

Here's the good part. Even if your natural tendency is that of a fixed mindset, know you are not doomed to the limited future that is typical for most of those with this perspective on the world. Now that you've been empowered with information around how the brain works and are aware of the limits of interpreting your possibilities through the limited lens of a "fixed" perspective you can intentionally begin to shift to a growth mindset. You can experience this shift by simply mastering the art of redirecting your thoughts. Remember, how you respond to situations is completely within your control. So the next time you face a challenge, experience a setback, or face criticism, know that these experiences are neither a reflection of your intelligence nor are they an arbiter of your capabilities.

Instead, ask yourself, "What can I learn from this?" Also, know that whatever skills you currently lack, can be acquired and eventually mastered. Simply put, there is no limit to what you can do.

Embrace Risk and Soar

When a major career opportunity required that Dorothy move to Wisconsin, she did so without knowing a soul. But with this risk, came great rewards in every aspect of her life. Within this new environment, she flourished both professionally and personally. She quickly moved up the corporate ranks at work, met her husband and started her family. At the end of the day, she had not only successfully faced the unknown, but before long, she had turned the unfamiliar into home in every sense of the word. Still, with this success, came new challenges, and before long, she knew something had to change.

She made the decision that she wanted to shift her life in a different direction, no longer wanting to work 60 plus hour work weeks. After distinguishing herself as a corporate leader, something for which she had worked and sacrificed for years, she made the conscious decision to step back, and focus on family. After becoming pregnant with her first child, Dorothy stepped off the corporate ladder, had her daughter and adopted a son. Some questioned the wisdom of this risky decision. But she knew this wasn't the end for her, it was merely a new beginning. Though the future was not guaranteed, her conscious life choice ultimately ended up being a pivotal turning point leading to her next area of exceptional success.

This former corporate executive who was previously making top-dollar, driving a company car, and working aggressive hours at work, now found herself with, as she puts it, 40-hour time slots she needed to fill. And so wisely, she never totally disappeared from the scene even though she was on a hiatus from her career. Instead, she became even more aggressively engaged in her community, volunteering with key organizations and assuming leadership roles in her sorority. By the time she was ready to take the necessary steps to reignite her career, she had created for herself a natural segue, becoming a liaison between the non-profit world and business industries by helping her corporate contacts recruit more people of color.

It was at this stage that she caught the attention of Goodwill Industries. And though she started off modestly, going from a major corporate salary to only $35,000 a year, she knew from the first day on the job that this would be the company from which she would retire. It was through this opportunity that all of her worlds united. Through Goodwill, Dorothy was able to merge business acumen with community service, and as a result, tap into her desire to give back on a daily basis. As an added bonus, the more sane pace gave her the space she needed in her life to be able to spend more time with her children and participate actively in their formative years.

Now, this doesn't mean that there weren't sacrifices along the way. But her willingness to bravely hit the reset button, coupled with the humbleness that it took to start again, and the diligence it required to learn an entirely new industry from the ground up, together, allowed her to be able to craft a life of *her* choosing and still end up on top.

Ultimately, Dorothy was able to apply her corporate expertise to a non-profit environment. This unique pairing and valuable skill-set meant that she stood out from the start and then swiftly rose through the ranks, eventually assuming the position of Sr. Vice President and overseeing a $400 million dollar enterprise.

While Dorothy's shift from a successful corporate career to re-inventing herself as a nonprofit leader did entail a significant level of risk, for most of us, professional risk-taking will not be as drastic. Much more common will be the "risk" of taking the lead on a critical project or choosing to focus your career in a high-stakes niche that carries with it a greater possibility for rewards. Even the "risk" of speaking up in a critical meeting and sharing an idea that breaks from the commonly espoused view, but one that adds value and lends a critical perspective that would have otherwise gone unexamined. All of these and more are examples of the types of risks you must be willing to take to distinguish yourself, be seen as a leader, and possibly become a game-changer in your industry. Yet, for many of us, risk is a powerful tool that consistently goes underutilized throughout our careers, and thus severely limits even the possibility of ground-breaking career advancement. Know this Sistahs, if you want to lead, the ability to assess and when appropriate, take calculated risks along the way, is a necessary part of the journey.

Former Wall Street Executive and current Head of Global Diversity for Bloomberg, Erika Brown, is crystal clear on the critical importance of risk-taking when it comes to maximizing career potential. In fact, she states emphatically,

"I try to encourage people to take risks and raise their hands. You can't wait for things to come to you. You have to have a plan. But there's your plan and then there's God's plan. And you have to have some faith in what God's plan is for you. You follow your plan to the extent that it gets you to the next step in God's plan. You have to be open-minded enough to be able to see opportunities when they're presented and you have to be prepared to seize those opportunities. Many times, that means taking a risk. And I think women of color are often very risk averse. In order to get to the next level, you have to take a risk. You have to have confidence in yourself. And that confidence can come through preparation, not just ego."

Certainly, Erika has tapped into a base truth here. The critical connection between risk and opportunity and the unfortunate reality of an increased aversion to risk taking among women of color, leaves us at a distinct disadvantage. Now, of course, it is likely true that there is a connection between a tendency towards risk aversion and the reality of greater personal, professional, and financial vulnerability among Black women that would account for our comparatively conservative nature when it comes to responding to potentially risky opportunities. It is, in fact, easier to take risks when you are confident that a safety net exists to catch you if you fall. For many of us, that safety net is completely non-existent. We are the most likely of all women in America to either be single or be the primary breadwinners in our homes. And though we're the most likely group of American women to work, when it comes to the level of wealth we've accumulated through our labor, the typical Black woman is virtually penniless. According to one study, our median wealth (meaning half of the Black women in America have more, and half have less) is only $100. That compares to over $41,000 held by White woman and over $12,000 held by Black men.[70] So for many of us, the stakes are higher. The risk vs. reward calculation takes on an entirely different hue when the potential for failure could go well past disappointment and straight into the realm of financial disaster.

The reality is, the different context that we face places us at an institutional disadvantage. The tightrope Black women uniquely walk, makes risk-taking an especially high stakes game for us, in essence, serving as an invisible inhibitor to our ability to feel free to take advantage of opportunities as they are presented. But if your goal is to pierce through to that next level of success, you must start putting in place now, your own personal and professional safety nets. That means, living below your means and amassing a financial cushion while also growing professional relationships that can help you properly assess "risks" as they arise. With these two pillars in place, you'll be equipped to boldly face opportunities knowing that you have the proper foundation to step forward and shine.

Be Willing to Put in the Work

If there is one constant I've found in my own life as well as in the lives of each of the exceptional women found throughout this book, it is the common willingness to *consistently* devote the time and effort necessary to succeed. Simply stated, uncommon results spawn from an uncommon commitment to consistent action. There's just no way around it. To distinguish yourself as a leader in your field, you must be willing to put in the work. So what does that look like? It means making a habit of engaging in the *daily* tasks that are necessary to produce results. So, for example, if you want to position yourself to stand out, get noticed, and get on the fast track in your career, one habit you might want to develop is that of showing up early—not on time—but actually early for work on a daily basis. Just think, if you began the daily practice of arriving to work a half hour early, what might be some of the cascading effects you would see? I'd suspect that over time, your productivity would substantially increase over where it is today and easily overtake that of others in your company, earning you the reputation of being a top producer. I'd also imagine that you'll have the opportunity to interact with and ultimately develop relationships with potential mentors and sponsors who will see your extra effort and come to appreciate your commitment and drive. With these built in advantages, when opportunities for advancement become available, guess who now stands a greater chance of being top of mind among decision-makers? Clearly, if there is one mindset shift that you can make right now that will exponentially increase your possibilities for the future, it is this—you must make the decision, right here and right now, that no one will out-hustle you. Once you turn hustle into a non-negotiable daily habit, success becomes an eventual inevitability.

Dee Marshall is one Sistah that seems to have hustle built into her DNA. A bundle of energy and positivity, Dee is one of those personalities that today, might have seemed destined for success. But her humble beginnings suggest that her future could have been anything but. Still, she had a hunger within her. A hunger that made her stand out. A hunger that took her from a modest secretarial school to Meryl Lynch. One that carried her from college to Wall Street. And a drive that led her to engage in meaningful work with Civil Rights Royalty, and then landed her in a power position at the New York Times. Her internal push continually opened doors for her, ultimately landing her a television show and a wildly successful life as an "accidental" entrepreneur. But at the root of it all, was the constant of hard work, buttressed by the intentional and consistent action of building strong connections with others. There is no way around it. To lead, you must be willing to put your skin in the game, do the work, and build relationships. With those constants in place opportunities will most certainly come.

"I understood that if it was a 9 to 5 and you showed up on time, you were late. You need to be early and leave late. People would tap me on the shoulder when jobs were available. I never had to

apply for a job. I wasn't that smart. I made okay grades, but what got me there was work ethic and emotional intelligence."

The level of professional commitment that Dee made habitual in her working life is precisely the type of commitment that gets noticed. And coupled with her intentional focus on maximizing her *emotional intelligence*, or ability to deeply and authentically connect with people, Dee was destined to stand out in her industry. The powerful combination of professional commitment and strong relationships allowed her to be top of mind when opportunities presented themselves and was the lynchpin that consistently propelled her to the top.

Much like Dee, Dara Richardson-Heron, President and CEO of YWCA of America, is quick to point out the critical component of hard work to those who aspire to leadership success. For Dara, it seemed, her natural leadership inclinations had always been there. Even at the tender age of two, she remembers attempting to lead her older sisters, but at least in those early days, things didn't go quite as expected. "One thing you know," she admits, "you're not that credible trying to lead people when you're in diapers!" Still, her parents saw within her the presence of strong leadership qualities, so they set about the task of helping her refine them. Top of their list however, was instilling in her in no uncertain terms the notion that "you kind of have to do something before you can lead."

So even as a child, Dara set her sights high. Ultimately, graduating second in her high school class, even completing college courses along the way. As she started along the path of obtaining her goal of becoming a doctor, she did so with extreme confidence that her academic success would continue. But it was at this stage in her life that she learned the tough lesson that not everything comes easy, even to someone as naturally gifted as her. And with this lesson, she gained an entirely new appreciation for the critical importance of the ability to face and conquer new challenges through the application of hard work.

"I came to college and took organic chemistry, a class you have to do well in to be considered for medical school. So I did my first exam and I got my blue book back and it had a red 12 on it. I

was thinking, it's 12 out of 15, 80 percent's not that bad. You can imagine my surprise when the professor said it was 12 out of 100. I just thought my life flashed before my eyes. It was devastating for me. But what it did, it gave me perspective. It let me know, the game is different now. And from that point on, my whole attitude changed. I knew I had to work much harder to be successful. It let me know that you've got to work hard. You can't rest on who you are. Even if you've been successful in previous things, it doesn't mean everything you touch turns to gold. You have to work really hard, even if you've achieved previous success."

Dara was able to take this lesson and apply it not only to her academic career but to the professional space. First as a medical doctor, then as a corporate leader, and currently as the leader of one of the world's biggest non-profits focused on improving the lives of women and eliminating racism around the world. But throughout the course of her career, she brought to each position, an authenticity to her leadership style that projected not only high expectations for her staff, but also, for herself, and a personal commitment to put in the work that's necessary to ensure those expectations are met.

Developing Your Own Leadership Mindset

Throughout this chapter we've examined specific characteristics inherent in the minds of successful Black women leaders. They are courageous, they are visionaries, and they are confident in their abilities to meet with success in the bold pursuit of their dreams. They take calculated risks to achieve uncommon rewards. And they put in the work, never shying away from undergoing the daily discipline that's necessary to one-day experience exceptional levels of success. Even when they've fallen short, they utilize the lessons that failure alone can provide to ultimately come back stronger, better prepared and more determined than ever before.

But now, what about you? How do you take this information and go from aspiration to application? How do you develop your own leadership mindset and use that transformation to acquire leadership success? The questions included in the *Exceptional Black Woman Vision and Action Guide* that follows will help you begin this process. But as you work through it, remember this: *Changing your mindset is not an instantaneous process. It's an evolution.* Like any other muscle in your body, to get stronger, you will need to instill new daily intentional actions to ensure that this shift takes hold. Start today by establishing your vision for your future. Be sure to make it a clear and vivid representation of your ultimate professional aspiration. Be as specific as possible. Identify not only what you'd like to achieve, but why. Becoming crystal clear about the motivation for your ambition is critical. This imperative will serve as your North Star as you push to make it through the tough times that absolutely everyone encounters along the way.

Next, develop a positive affirmation that will serve as your daily reminder that with applied effort, belief in yourself, and the gift of consistency, you will, one day, make it to the top. Your affirmation can sound something like the following:

> *"Within (years/months), I will (insert goal here). I know I can achieve this goal. Within me lies the ability to develop the skills necessary to make my vision a reality. If I fall short at any point along the way, I will love myself enough to exhibit the gift of self-compassion. I realize that set-backs are a natural part of the learning process, and as such, are a foundational element to eventual success. I commit to learn the lessons that are entangled in these experiences and then come back stronger and better prepared to achieve my destined success. Today I commit to the daily actions of courage, commitment, confidence and hard work because I know it is through the consistent application of each of these principles that I will one day move from dream to reality."*

Remember, to get from where you are now to where you want to go, the first, and most foundational element that you must master is the ability to free your mind from whatever is currently holding you back from being your absolute best. If it's fear, you must find the courage to let it go. If it's lack of confidence, you must identify the greatness within you and consistently remind yourself of your unique brilliance. If it's a deficiency in a specific critical skill set, you must commit to the work that's necessary to master that which currently holds you back.

To evolve into the leader you are fully capable of becoming, take a moment right now to get crystal clear about your ultimate professional goals, then commit yourself to the actions that are necessary to get there. With a strong work ethic, comes strengthened ability. With stellar ability comes confidence, and with confidence comes the habit of obliterating fear. With these qualities in place, you must then commit yourself to the practices that are necessary to build the necessary financial cushion to allow you the freedom to be able to take advantage of appropriate professional risks when they present themselves. As a result, you will be better equipped to make use of the full range of opportunities that come your way. But most importantly, you must always remember that you already have within you everything you need to be able to acquire whatever is necessary to achieve your boldest, most audacious visions of success.

Before moving forward, complete the exercise at the end of this chapter, and then commit to at least one *daily* action that will get you closer to your dream. It is through this process of vision followed by consistent strategic action that you will build the necessary momentum for your eventual success.

Exceptional Black Woman Vision & Action Guide

1. At the end of Chapter 1, you identified your biggest and boldest professional ambition. Why is that goal important to you? In other words, what will make all the effort that will be necessary to achieve it worthwhile?

2. Often opportunity comes wrapped up in an element of risk. What actions can you take now, to prepare yourself to be able to leap if such an opportunity were to arise?

3. ASSIGNMENT: Type out the affirmation included in this chapter, complete with your specific goal and time limitation. Purchase a beautiful frame in which to display your affirmation and place it in one of your favorite spots in your home. Remember to recite it daily. Speak it, until you believe it.

CHAPTER 4

Cracking the Corporate Code

❝ For women of color, there are the rules and then there are the rules. The secret rules are that there are no rules. They can do what they want to do. If I were to do it again, there were times when I would have pushed more for myself. And when the answer came back, I would have pushed again. ❞

—Denise Evans, MBA
Vice President, IBM Corporation

B y any measure imaginable, IBM Vice President, Denise Evans has built a career reflective of exceptional success. Having reached the exclusive ranks of executive leadership at one of the most prestigious corporations in the world, this native Washingtonian created a life for herself that most could only imagine. Still, her path to this space has been anything but easy. Although she grew up in a loving family and protective community, Denise personally experienced the turmoil and "ugly stuff" of desegregation. From there, she distinguished herself as an academic achiever, ultimately collecting two Ivy League degrees including an MBA from Stanford. But her path to success, like all of the corporate leaders who share their wisdom in this chapter, was far from preordained. Even among the most privileged, distinguishing yourself in the corporate environment is far from easy. But for a Black woman, carving a path to stand-out in the ultra-competitive and high-stakes environment that is Corporate America takes a multitude of qualities, strategies, and actions that must be properly aligned and expertly implemented to dodge the distinct hurdles that are sure to come specifically your way. Still, know that with all you must do and be to excel in this, perhaps the most competitive of work environments, it all starts with merely one thing—a plan.

Plan Your Career

Shellye Archambeau, CEO of MetricStream, is a born planner. The daughter of a corporate executive, she knew early on that she wanted to create for herself a future as a business leader. So in high school, Shellye put in place the fundamentals of a plan that would accelerate her path to success. She knew, for example, that the University of Pennsylvania's Wharton School of Business was the top Business School in the nation, and so she applied there and only there. It was her belief that with a degree from Wharton, she could forgo an MBA, and instead achieve her leadership dreams on an accelerated timetable. The day she learned of her acceptance to her top (and only) college choice, was the day her long-term success-plan was initiated. Over the years, her penchant for carefully researching and thus clearly understanding key prerequisites for success, and then developing a plan birthed from that due diligence, ultimately payed off for her, again and again. Still, according to Shellye, a plan alone, no matter how sound and no matter how necessary, is simply not enough.

"The key is to realize that a plan is just that—a plan. You update it and refine it based on new information, so it's a living, breathing thing. And a plan is not worth very much if you haven't broken it down into time-defined goals. Because if you have a time limit on it, it will force you to act. So for example, I was working for IBM in Harrisburg, Pennsylvania and I was driving toward my goal, which was to be a Business Unit Executive by the time I was thirty. Now, IBM was going through a tough time. And although I was doing a lot of team leadership, I wasn't on track. So I told them I was willing to move for more opportunity. Harrisburg is obviously a small market, I didn't have to

stay there. I was doing well. I was ranked and rated very well. I was definitely told I had the skills and capabilities, but there just weren't any opportunities open yet. Well, tick-tock, tick-tock. If I didn't get the next job soon, it's no way I'm going to meet my goal within the timeframe. So I said, you know what? I wanted to work at IBM, and I wanted to run a business at IBM, but perhaps it's not a good idea, because I don't see how I'm going to get my goal met while I'm here. So I looked for opportunities outside and I found an opportunity that would put me on track. And so I came back and told them I was leaving. And they were shocked!"

"So, long story short, I met my goal. And it turned out that my boss hadn't told people. You know, I told him that I was willing to move and willing to do other things, but I wasn't being considered for roles outside of the Harrisburg market. Now you can say that's sexism or racism, or that he just wanted to keep me because I was performing, but you don't know, right? But the point is, if I hadn't had a time limit on it, it would've been easy to get stuck. I was doing well, making money, and getting positive feedback. It's really comfortable just to stay and wait. That's why it's so important to have time defined guidelines on it. If I'd waited, I may not be where I am right now."

And where she is right now is not merely the leader of a business unit, but the CEO of an entire organization. But this too, did not come without careful planning, ground-breaking implementation of that plan, and the courage and flexibility to strategically make adjustments along the way. For Shellye, from the moment she started her career, she knew she not only wanted to lead, she wanted to become a CEO. And so, as she has done consistently, she made situational assessments, took note of what others had done to advance, and then devised a plan to make her goals a lived reality. Realizing her CEO aspiration was no different, she went about the task of plotting her path. Here's how she did it:

"My research had shown that every single CEO at IBM started out in sales. So that's part of executing the plan and I get commission! Plus, if I can do this well, I can pay off my student loans

faster, and I did. So, that's where I started, and then I fairly quickly moved up the chain, between sales and then management and ultimately business unit executive and then into the executive role. So I ended up leveraging my experiences not only in sales but also in marketing. Because one of the things I realized was that IBM had about 200,000 employees, and all of them probably want to be CEO, so how could I differentiate myself? Marketing was one of my concentration areas when I was at Wharton, so I thought, 'I can become good at marketing and maybe that could help differentiate me.' And that worked out well. My first executive role was actually a marketing role—it was the Global Director for Market Management."

"From there, I took on a couple of roles and ended up over at Asia Pacific. Again, part of my objective, because it appeared every line executive who worked for the CEO at IBM, did a stint, not just internationally, but in Japan. I was the Vice President and General Manager and was responsible for a multi-billion dollar division. And at that point, there wasn't anyone who looked like me. There were no African American females higher than me in the company. But ultimately, I decided two things. I wasn't happy with my compensation at IBM, and I also was getting concerned about what roles would I really want when I went back? And though at that point it seemed I was only two steps away [from the CEO position], in actuality, I was many steps away in terms of building out the overall grooming that it takes. So even though I loved IBM, I mean if you cut me, I probably bled blue because of my whole experience, I opened myself up to opportunity. And I decided I could go run a smaller company where I could have a real impact and build something. So I again did my research and learned that many people who go from running business units and divisions in big companies to running smaller companies failed a time or two, because it's just very different. And I know, or at least have always felt, that as an African American female, I don't have as many strikes at bat as other people do. And that's why I always try to increase my odds for success by doing my research and putting together a

plan. So I decided to go and take a couple of Officer level roles, you know, seat at the table kind of roles so I could understand what's different, and then go after my CEO role. And that's what I did. I was recruited to be President of blockbuster.com back when they launched their very first website back in the late 1990's. And then I was recruited to Silicon Valley and became the Chief Marketing Officer and VP of Sales at a telecommunications company that was ultimately sold to AT&T. And then held the same role at LoudCloud, and then was hired to be the CEO of my current firm."

What's critical to learn about Shellye's experience is that she was very methodical about her path to leadership. At each stage along the way, she studied the prerequisites to success by determining key roles and credentials others had acquired who held the position to which she aspired. And with that critical information in mind, she developed an action plan—one that followed the formula that had already proven to be a gateway to success. But perhaps even more critical was her understanding that plans need specific time limitations and, at times significant adjustments. She was not shy about letting others know about her aspirations, and when they didn't move on that information, she was prepared to do so herself. And finally, when it became clear to her that her original goal of becoming CEO of IBM would probably not be the right fit for her, she didn't lose sight of her base aspiration. Instead, she opened herself up to new opportunities and once again, began to think strategically to determine, if not IBM, then what CEO position would be best for her? Once the decision was made to lead a smaller company instead, she followed her same planning formula to craft a path to leadership success.

Clearly, Shellye is a brilliant woman with an amazing work ethic and a strong commitment to her career. But what made her reach the levels of success that she has experienced has been her propensity to plan her career, stay committed to her ultimate goal, and still embrace the flexibility that's necessary to ultimately move from aspiration to actuality.

Over-Deliver and Self-Promote

While taking the time to plan your career is foundational to fulfilling your future ambitions, where the rubber really meets the road is in your ability to deliver on a daily basis *and* get credit for your contributions. In Corporate America especially, delivering consistent, high-quality results is an essential precursor to putting yourself on the career fast-track. Keeping in mind too, that as a Black woman, fair or not, you may indeed have to not only deliver, but, over-deliver. The old adage is true. Being just as good as your peers is often not good enough. In many situations, you'll have to be better. And then you must understand how to tactfully raise your profile such that you become a known entity in your professional space, and as such, receive due credit for the work that you do and the opportunities for advancement that you deserve.

Denise Evans, of IBM, understands this principle well and shares its critical importance:

"When you come to Corporate America, be number 1 at what you do. Learn the business. Develop yourself to be the best. Nobody remembers the guy that came in 4th. We don't promote on personality; we promote on results. Number 1, 2 and 3 are consistently high performing. Consistent high performance works for everyone. But for women and people of color, even that's not enough. Do a good job, yes. Be good, yes. But you also have to promote yourself."

Bernadette Noland, Talent Development Director for Saks Fifth Avenue, understands well the fine balance between consistent stellar performance and the necessity of self-promotion. For her, in fact, the two go hand-in-hand.

"My work ethic has always been there, even from when I was 14 years old, working at the ice cream stand. When I put my all into something, I literally give 150-200%. So I make sure I interface with people that recognize that. Even for those that don't recognize that, I make sure that they do. And it's in a way that's very subtle. It's not necessarily arrogant or anything of that nature.

The other piece too, considering my background culturally, and all of the historical things that go along with being an African American woman, I think a large part of it is stepping up and asking for what I want. I'll give you an example. Right now I'm in a position where I am promotable, given the work that I've done at Sax thus far. So my next role will be the Regional HR Director role. And so one of the things that I've done is that I've stepped up with my current Regional to let her know that I'd like some special assignments. So yesterday, she was unable to host our weekly call, and that's about seventeen stores in our region, so I hosted it. She offered me the opportunity to host the call. I also have the opportunity to go to New York and shadow her during what we call our regional meet. That's an opportunity to interface with a lot of the Executive Vice Presidents and Vice Presidents to get additional exposure. And so I think it's important not necessarily to sit back and wait for someone to see your success. It's not advantageous at all to wait for someone to offer you something. You got to step up, and you've got to ask for it."

Remember, a stellar work ethic, and top performance are both necessary for your journey to leadership, but as important as these qualities are, they are not sufficient to get you where you are capable of going. Do the work. Be a consistent top performer and then take the next step. To break out of the Black girl bubble that could keep you indefinitely in a suspended state of isolation, you've got to become intentional about reaching out, expressing your ambitions, and making sure that the right people are aware of both your abilities and your ambitions.

Vanessa De Luca, Editor-in-Chief of Essence Magazine, understands the critical importance of getting on the radar screen of key decision makers as a precursor to advancement. Though she now sits atop the nation's leading magazine aimed at the African American woman, her success in acquiring the position came only after two previous unsuccessful attempts. She knew she was well-prepared to do the job successfully. Having worked at Essence for a dozen years, she'd contributed to virtually every department in the organization.

As such, she understood well every aspect of the business. Still, she knew, at least, the first time around, that her attempt at becoming Editor-in-Chief would most likely not be successful because not enough people knew who she was. But she didn't let that stop her. In fact, she threw her hat in the ring anyway to put herself on their radar screen. Now, while she didn't land the top spot on the first go round, she did receive the number two position, Executive Editor of the magazine. Not a bad outcome in the least. When reflecting on the situation Vanessa admits,

> *"I already knew it wasn't going to happen, and I said, 'Maybe this is not the right time for me anyway. But I'll never get to that point if I don't make sure that the people who are in the decision-making process know who I am."*

It was this willingness to position herself in front of key decision-makers that helped to raise awareness about Vanessa's capabilities and ultimately led to her eventual success. Years later, after transitioning from Essence, when the opportunity presented itself again, she was now not only a known entity, she was the obvious choice for the top spot.

Vanessa warns,

> *"A lot of people say, 'They should know that I'm ambitious. They should know that I want to be a manager.' But do they really know that? I mean, have you told them that?"*

And as some of her earlier experiences show, "telling them that," doesn't always require verbal communication. Prior to joining Essence, Vanessa served for a period of time as a writer for Glamour magazine. While there, she noticed that her manager would often look at things on her desk. Vanessa used that tendency to relay her ambitions in a rather non-traditional way.

> *"One day, I wrote a list of the next five things I wanted to do in the next six months. And so a couple of days later, we had a check-in meeting, and she brought out a couple of things that were on my*

desk. And now I see, you know what I want. She mentioned two things on that list that I did not have to verbally tell her. I put it on her radar, and she wanted to keep me happy. She even made it look like it was her idea. You've got to let people know what you want. They have so much going on. They have a million people to manage. If there's something you really want, you have to let the right people know it. My mom always says, 'If you don't ask, you don't get.' "

Assemble Your Career Dream Team

By now you know it's critical to plan your career. And you also know that your plan must be buttressed by a habit of over-delivering. But we've also established that performing well consistently, as important as it is, ultimately won't be of much good to your future if the right people aren't made aware of your stellar performance. As such, it's your responsibility to let them know. Express your ambitions, position yourself to be considered for next-level opportunities, and grow relationships that will serve you well in the days to come. It's this last piece that harkens to the next essential element of extraordinary success—the formulation of your own Career Dream Team.

If you're like most, you already understand the critical importance of developing good mentoring relationships. And we'll soon address exactly how to go about achieving that goal. But also understand that even with the right mentors in place, you need additional support. The fact of the matter is, no one achieves high levels of success alone. No one. So embrace the notion that it takes teamwork to make the dream work. And be aggressive and selective about comprising the team that will be instrumental to your success.

When making decisions around your Career Dream Team know that it should be broad and inclusive of specific key individuals. In addition to mentors it should also include advocates or sponsors, coaches, and current and former managers. In other words, you want to include those who know your skills, talents, and career aspirations, and who can give you honest feedback, insight, and support throughout your career.

Your mentors will provide you with regular guidance along your career path and as such, will help you move forward more efficiently and effectively than you ever could alone. In contrast, personal interaction with advocates or sponsors will be infrequent, if not absolutely non-existent. But they know enough about you, your ambitions, and your capabilities that they can advocate effectively on your behalf behind closed doors in key decision-making situations that can directly influence your career ascension possibilities.

Coaches can help you improve or develop specific essential skill sets along the way. They can also provide assistance in helping you develop an overarching career game-plan and then serve as a consistent source of accountability and feedback as you go about the task of implementation.

And finally, current and former managers can provide invaluable insight on your performance and if so moved, can actively take you under their wing to ensure you have critical experiences and exposure to others who can be crucial to your future success.

Assembling your Career Dream Team may seem daunting. So set your sights on first developing good mentoring relationships as they can serve as the linchpin toward helping to identify and bring on board your full roster of career support.

Karie Conner, Regional Sales Director for Nike, accelerated her path to success by understanding the relationship between hard work and the support of a broad network of mentors. She knew literally from day one that Corporate America was the right fit for her professionally, but she also learned that not everyone shared her ambition. That realization provided the opportunity for her to stand out. So through her own grit and with the help of a broad network of mentors, she's been able to advance quickly in her career.

"I saw opportunity in my job to grow my business, and I was really excited and super passionate about what I was doing. So I knew right away, I couldn't be like [others] were. I knew right away I wasn't the type of person who was going to just do what I have to do to get by because I've never been that person. My parents have never told me, you should just do what you have to do to

get by. They always told me, work really hard and if you love what you do, you'll never work a day in your life. So for me, I knew rather quickly that I had to separate myself from that, and I did. I concentrated on doing what I loved. Telling the stories of what we were trying to do and sell and grow my business and find creative avenues to do so. So it's kind of funny. I think if I'd started with a group of people who all wanted to work hard and grow their businesses and stand out and shine, I may have not grown as fast in my career as I have. But [standing out] set me up for success."

"In the meantime, I also learned how much mentorship was important. I started to really pay attention to the people who will help me [advance] and give me the experiences that I need to be successful. I have continued to make sure that I seek out those people; it's almost like forming an allyship. I have my people quarterly, my people monthly, and my people bi-monthly that I speak with that range all the way up throughout the company and even my peers as well to continue to make sure that I'm checking in and checking on my skill sets to make sure that I'm setting myself up for success."

"In my career path, I've worked on a lot of different businesses even within the sales functions and along the way I've learned different things from different people. That person is very data oriented, there's something from them that I can gain. That person is very left-brained, and they think very creatively, so I like how they think, and I think there's something I can gain from that person. And then there's diversity in race, gender, sexuality, it ranges all the way throughout. But what I've definitely learned is that there's always something that someone has a talent for that they can share with me that may address a weakness or expand an opportunity, and it definitely helps."

Appreciating the talents, skills, and abilities that others have is one thing. But actually attracting them such that they agree to be your mentor, is quite another. For many, it's this critical issue that's the stumbling block to forming those mentoring relationships that are critical for success. For Karie, it's all about observation and then having the courage to ask.

"I'm always observing and paying attention, when I'm sitting in a meeting for example. And I didn't always do that. I was always kind of scared to talk to some of these people. People who were up in front of the whole company talking to everybody. When you're younger in the company, you don't think you'll ever be that person up there. They're like a celebrity in their own right. But then you realize, they're just a normal person too. Once I got over that hump and realized it, I felt very comfortable going to anyone and just saying, 'Hey, I want to seek mentorship with you.' And I tell everyone, you can never have enough mentors, because everyone has something different they can share with you."

"There have been times when I've reached out to people via e-mail and introduced myself. And then there have been times when I've been in a bathroom and they've come out of the bathroom. Or I'm sitting at the lunch table with them or I'm in a meeting with them. There was a point in time when I wouldn't say anything, I would just say, 'Hi.' But then I kind of had to have a talk with myself and say, if you want something, if you want to get after it, then you need to talk to these people because they can be helpful. And I think it was me learning through talking to other people who wanted to mentor me and I wanted them to mentor me as well. They kind of coached me there too. Hey, you should talk to so and so, they're good at this, or you have that in common with this person. And so I think it was just me getting more familiar with the fact that I did have something in common with the President of North America because she played basketball in college too. Or there's another person that just had a daughter and that child is 18 months too. You know just finding those commonalities makes you feel a little bit more at ease. But it kind of got to that point where, you don't lose anything by introducing yourself and talking to somebody. It's about getting more comfortable in your own skin and knowing that, what do you have to lose? It's one of those things where you lose nothing, but you can gain everything."

While Karie has been exceedingly successful in gaining mentors through a direct approach by simply asking for mentorship, for others, mentorship acquisition requires a lighter touch. Erika Brown, Global Head of Diversity and Inclusion at Bloomberg, emphasizes the importance of first focusing on relationship development as an alternative to the more direct approach to mentor acquisition that worked so well for Karie. For her, it's all about developing relationships that have depth, and therefore, have staying power over time.

> *"The one thing that's a major turn off for me, is when people are transactional: 'I want you to be my mentor.' It's like asking someone to marry you before dating them. I do think it's important that relationships grow over time. There can be a situation where the company assigns mentors, and it's important to be a part of the corporate culture and help others be successful in the corporate culture in which you work. But also, relationships happen over time. So I'm still mentoring the young lady that started working for me in 2005 at Lehman Brothers. Relationships grow, and they last if they're substantial. One of my biggest problems nowadays when people ask me to mentor them, is not that I don't want to, it's that I haven't given up any of my other mentees...because the type of person I am. You also have to consider that when people are evaluating mentors, most are going to be pretty busy people. And it's okay to be busy. The people that have the most to do, do the most, right? So it's not just about being busy, but at the same time, you want people that can devote the time and effort to it. When I don't feel like I can devote the proper time and effort to a relationship or a project, that's when I have to make the tough decisions. So when I think about taking on additional mentees, I have to think about whether or not I really have the capacity to support that type of relationship that I would take very seriously."*

It's this approach that's based on growing relationships through less formal interactions over time which proved to be successful for MetricStream CEO, Shellye Archambeau. Of course, as a high performer, she was matched with a company mentor early on, and so she received formal mentorship through this system. But Shellye also admits, most of her mentors, didn't even know they were her mentor. She just treated them that way.

"When you ask people to be a mentor, they lean back, they close in, they're thinking time commitment and they say no. I just do an 'Oh, by the way' question. And then I do what they suggest or a version of it, and then I get back to them. And I tell them, you told me to do XYZ and I did it, and I really appreciate it. So then what does that do? They feel good. Maybe a quarter later, I reach back out for a quick thought, 'What do you think...?' If you do that, and it goes well, and you get back to them, they ultimately want to claim you as you demonstrate success. I cannot tell you the number of people who have asked for advice from me and I never hear from them again. They'll reach out, ask for advice and then they disappear. Relationships have to be two-way."

For Denise Evans, of IBM, it was Shellye who was not just her mentor, but a key sponsor who opened up the pathway for her first opportunity to ascend to executive leadership. Shellye was well aware of Denise's ambitions as well as her capabilities. With that knowledge in hand, when the right opportunity was on the horizon, it was Shellye who made sure it was Denise who would be positioned to move up.

"She's in Japan and I get a call from her. She gets right to the point. She says, 'Look, there's an opportunity that I think you'd be the best executive for. I'm going to give the decision-makers your name.' I told her, [my current boss] wants to keep me here. Sometimes you're such a high performer, people want to keep you on their team, and they don't want you to leave. She coached me through that. I get offered the job, my first executive position, and she goes, 'I knew you would get it. That was the perfect job for you. You're number two and number three is going to drop next week. I have a commitment to myself to get six women a year into an executive position.' I asked her if that was required for

her position? She said, 'No. That's just what I do.' And I was like,
'You're not even halfway through the year.'"

"*The point is I got my first executive position in a top spot*
because she was behind closed doors in those conversations, or
she was seeking out opportunities, and she had specific people in
mind. Don't just plan your career, tell strategic people what your
aspirations are. Tell people, 'I'm looking to get promoted.' 'I'm
looking for my next executive position.' She was an advocate for
me. That's what advocates do. Advocates advocate for you behind
closed doors when you don't even know."

Ensuring that your Career Dream Team is filled with a range
of mentors either formally asked or informally drafted, as well as
sponsors who know your capabilities and ambitions and are willing
to advocate on your behalf, is critical to your future success. With
your team in tow, there is literally no limit to how far you can go.

Network Like a BOSS

One of the best ways to get on the radar screen of potential advocates
and mentors, as well as gain insider knowledge and better overall
traction both within your specific company as well as within your career generally, is to become a master of networking. What's important
to keep in mind is that networking is so much more than attending
specific pre-orchestrated "networking events" and amassing an impressive collection of business cards. Networking like a *BOSS* requires
developing a professional lifestyle, within which you incorporate habits that continually provide opportunities for you to meet new people,
develop and strengthen mutually beneficial relationships, and even at
times, gain access to critical insider information precisely because of
those actions. Looked at from this three-pronged perspective, it's easy
to see why effective networking is an absolutely essential component
of any successful strategy that ultimately results in maximizing your
chances at extraordinary success.

I always advise my clients to think of networking as a multi-layered
activity. It requires actions that are primarily based within your current
organization, actions that must occur external to your organization,

> "You can sit back and wait for things to happen or you can make things happen."

but are focused within your professional sphere, and broader inter-disciplinary associations that can connect you to a large and diverse range of talents, skills, and expertise that may one day be personally useful if you ever decide to switch gears professionally or as a resource that can be tapped into to assist others within your network. Once you've built an extensive collection of relationships that are reflective of both an internal and external network, then you will begin to see, in multiple ways, just how crucial these relationships are and can be when it comes to actually living your greatest potential.

Right out of graduate school, Denise noticed that her colleagues at IBM made it their business to engage in networking activities. It was through these after-work events that she received critical information that ultimately helped her advance her career and guard against discriminatory acts. Through these informal channels she was able to determine if her pay was on par with her peers and discover which assignments would result in the biggest rewards. But perhaps her biggest observation from being active in this way was understanding that even in these informal environments she was still being watched and ultimately, being assessed for her level of ambition and professional potential.

> *"They're looking not only at your professional attributes, but are you a player? If you want to move up in Corporate America, you have to play to win. You can sit back and wait for things to happen, or you can make things happen. I understood that as an introvert, I needed to start being out there. There would be times when people would go out for drinks, and though I don't drink, I would always go. I remember someone coming by and saying, you're a player aren't you? He was observing me. Am I staying in a corner or am I interacting with people?"*

This point is critical. You've got to find the courage to push through your inner introvert to win at this game, knowing that your actions are signaling to others your commitment to advancement within the company. You've got to show you want it. And part of that demonstration is not only doing what needs to be done inside professional spaces, but also showing up and taking part in more informal professional interactions. It's through this kind of commitment that you demonstrate you're one of the team. And you too, have what it takes to score.

Charisse Lillie, President of the Comcast Foundation made one simple decision early on in her career that ultimately helped her to expand her network quickly and effectively. Implementing just this one simple practice, when utilized consistently, can open you up to developing a broad range of new relationships, literally, from day one.

> *"I would never sit next to someone that I know. I would always sit next to someone I didn't know. It might be uncomfortable, but you do things to break the ice and then, follow up with them. You've got to meet people half way. Sometimes people are resistant or shy, you meet them more than half way, you go 60 percent. But it's worth it, because any opportunity you have to get to know people, you should take. At a place like Comcast, where you have 150,000 employees, we have employee resource groups, and any kind of internal networking that your company offers, you need to take advantage of. You've got to have an internal network of support as well as an external network."*

For Charisse, an attorney by training, much of her external network was developed by way of professional organizational involvement. An active member of the American Bar Association, the National Bar Association, and the Barrister's Association of Philadelphia, among others, Charisse has grown broad and strong connections not only inside Comcast, but also, outside of her work environment. And these connections have paid off in numerous ways. One, which actually came by way of her husband's network, even led to her appointment as Chair of the Board for the Federal Reserve of Philadelphia.

> *"The General Counsel to the Federal Reserve Bank was a Kappa brother of my husband. He [gained the support of] the sitting Chair of the Federal Reserve and recommended me [for the position]. I*

had these two folks that were vouching for me, creating this opportunity, and I ended up being Chair of the Board."

Jotaka Eaddy, Sr. Vice President of Government Affairs for Silicon Valley-based PayNearMe, Inc. truly lives the importance of valuing her network by moving beyond the notion of merely developing transactional relationships, but instead, building meaningful relationships based on authenticity and mutual respect.

"My biggest asset is my network. You need to treat your network like a piece of stock. It is valuable. It's absolutely essential. It's a difference between treating your network like it's a tool vs. it's valuable. To me, the relationships that I have are very valuable. I may not ask them, can you do this for me. It's I'd just like to talk to you, because your life experience has been extremely helpful in my growth. Being in the presence of people is often more important than transactional things. So for me, I make it a point to stay in touch. To just check in, because I sincerely want to know, how'd they do it? If you are authentic in your relationships, I think your network and the richness of your network grows. Because I actually really care about how they're feeling. And when you really care, it shows."

What Jotaka emphasizes is the one critical component of networking that far too many miss. Networks are about much more than just an endless stream of contacts stored neatly in a cell phone. And it's certainly more than merely a real-life application of six degrees of separation. True networks, are about growing and nurturing relationships, and taking the time to really get to know the people to whom you are connected. It's only by going the extra mile by really growing and nurturing authentic relationships that your network will have the chance to fully blossom, strengthen, and ultimately, grow into all that it has the potential to be.

Neutralize the Angry Black Woman Perception

At the heart of leadership is having the ability to articulate a vision such that others buy into it, work consistently towards it, and at the end of the day, produce results. Now an integral part of that equation involves setting goals and timetables and holding people accountable for their part of the collective responsibility to get things done. Problem is, what looks and sounds like leadership coming from a man, can be interpreted completely differently, coming from a woman. And for a Black woman, having to navigate the well-worn cultural stereotype of the "Angry Black Woman" means that while just like your colleagues, you're responsible for holding your team accountable for results, your directives may elicit a very different response than they would if they were to come from someone else.

In dealing with this conundrum, it's important to understand how to communicate in a way that elicits respect in spite of the extra burden you bear. And if there are a set of commonalities around how exceptionally successful Black women in corporate environments have risen to this challenge it is this: Be fair. Be firm. Be in control of your tone and facial expressions. And above all else, never let them see you sweat.

Erika of Bloomberg acknowledges that she's naturally the type of person who smiles when she speaks, no matter what she's saying. And she believes that smile helps to defuse situations. But even with this natural inclination on her side, she doesn't shy away from communicating sternly when that's what the situation calls for.

"There are some situations where you're meant to be stern about things. But even in that discourse, I'm a professional. So how you handle things professionally is important. You can be firm, and you can disagree without coming across as angry. Just like what your mother said, it's not what you say, it's how you say it."

Like Erika, Shellye too often laces what she has to say with a smile, but that doesn't mean the substance of her message is any less direct than it needs to be to get results. She admits,

"I'm assertive and direct with a smile. Say what you need to say, and then smile because it's easier to take. I try very hard to control my emotions. People will describe me as, 'Shellye is very calm,

and she's very together.' You've got to be a duck on the pond. The duck on the pond looks like it's gliding around easily, but under water, its feet are moving like crazy. You've got to be the same way. You've got to establish confidence in people."

"My leadership style starts with clarity, strong communication around vision and objectives and then ensuring that people understand what they need to do and they understand why; why it's good for the company and why it's good for them. I'm a big believer in coaching and developing people. And then you have to have a plan, and hold people accountable for executing."

As for Charisse of Comcast, the concern is less about perceptions and more about getting results.

"I'm unapologetic about having standards, having goals and meeting those goals. I never want to be rude or disrespectful to people, but there are times when you have to be direct and clear. I see that there are times when you're very clear, but people still don't hear what you have to say. You don't have to drive a stake in people's heart to be effective. You have to be firm, stand your ground, and not be bullied. Nobody's going to bully me."

Reflecting back on her corporate career, International President of Alpha Kappa Alpha Sorority, Inc., Dr. Dorothy Buckhanan Wilson admits,

"People want us to be polite and kind and deferential in a lot of situations. But women have to speak up and have a firm sense of self. I'm not saying be angry. I'm not saying yell. But certainly, make sure that people know that if you come over here, with whatever it is that you're coming with today, understand that you're going to have someone who's going to let you know what's going on. Someone who's going to be very clear and very precise around what kind of conversation we're going to have today. And a part of it, I think is that because a lot of us have not been really conditioned to deal with confrontation or to deal with

challenges in the workplace, in a way that does not involve us raising our voices, it does get to be frustrating. The beauty of age, like once you get over age 45, or just being older at this point, is that I know how to talk in a tone. I can be very low in the corner talking to you, and saying the things where most people have no idea what I'm saying, but not change my facial expression, and not change my approach. I don't show what it is but the person I'm dealing with knows exactly where I'm coming from. They get the message loud and clear. But a lot of our younger women haven't quite yet perfected that. It comes with fine-tuning and polishing, but you got to be in situations where you can have those crucial conversations with individuals that you're interacting with, where you're doing it at a level, or you're doing it in a tone in which you don't come across as the 'angry Black woman.'"

"But sometimes, despite your best efforts, you're going to come across that by virtue of the fact that you pushed back, that you said something back. Some days you don't say anything. But some days you have to say, hmmm, not quite so sure. Let's look at this another way. Can we turn this over? Can we offer another perspective? Look at things a little different? But I think a part of it is that we do have to be able to say that we have a voice. We have been major contributors in this country. Women, especially women of color, helped build this country. And so we're not just going to sit by and let you say anything about us. We are going to have a lot more to say about who we are, but we're going to say it in a way where you'll clearly understand it. We're also going to say it in a way in which you're going to understand that we're not going to take just anything that someone else decides that they're going to push out there on us. I'm going to have a firm, positive interaction with you, but we're going to have that crucial conversation. And you need to be willing to listen."

"The reality is, we are living in diverse times. We're not only in a diverse nation, we're in a diverse world. And people are going to have to learn how to deal with it. Today, it's African American women. Tomorrow it's going to be some other group. They're going to have to learn how to deal with people

that are different. And there are a lot of things that are happening out here, and we're not making it up. People do—a lot of times, you walk up on them, and they do and say things that are insensitive, and they're not aware that you have to do a lot more thinking when you're dealing with people of color. And that's real. That's not in your mind. So some days, we do have something to be angry about. But we just have to understand how to have those conversations."

Denise shares her method for defusing potentially, highly charged situations so that you can respond in a way that's effective and ultimately allows you to be truly heard. It's called, the "Three Breath Rule."

"Take three breaths and really think about what you'd like to say. Think about what it'd look like if it were on the front page of your hometown newspaper. Then think about a diplomatic way of saying it. Because if nothing else, never let them see you sweat. The minute you lose your temper, you've lost the argument. Even if you're 'right' people won't listen. They become defensive, and you've lost."

Successfully Navigate the 'isms in the Corporate Space

Having experienced not only racism and sexism in her career but also the sting of colorism, Dorothy suggests that having to confront racism and sexism and more in the workplace are in some situations, all but inevitable. But with the right anecdote, you can still land on top.

"When you're a six foot tall, left handed, dark-skinned African American woman like me, you'll see everything. I've been in places that it's in your face 24/7. I've experienced less subtle forms, but most of it was pretty blatant. Throughout my career, I've always cultivated networks. No matter what you're going through, if you talk to people who've been through something similar, they

can help you deal with it. There were people further up the food chain at Johnson Wax that helped me negotiate those situations."

"They tend to get us on writing skills, communications skills, or our work-ethic. Those three things, I was impeccable. You're not going to outwork me. And my writing and communications skills are impeccable. The minute they found out they could not mess with you in those areas, then people realized they have to deal with you on your terms. If you deliver consistent results, at the end of the day, that's what drives the company. They may not like you, but if you get results, you're going to be a force to be reckoned with."

Similarly, Karie's experience in the corporate space has shown her that nothing speaks quite like results. Though she's often felt others assumed she'd acquired her position merely because she's a Black woman, over time, she has become quite comfortable with and confident in her abilities. Ultimately, she knows she's good at what she does, so when those occurrences happen, she refuses to entertain the notion.

"I have felt it numerous times where somebody thinks I got a job because I'm a Black woman and not by my abilities. And I've felt, at times, that I've had to prove myself to show that, no, I am good at what I do and that's why I'm here. Cause you hear people say things sometimes like, 'Oh, you know the company is pushing this to happen right now...' But then at the same time, I've become confident in my abilities. I know that I'm very good at what I do and things I'm not confident in, I'm going to go to people to help me. So I've actually learned to just forget about that part and act like it doesn't exist. I don't know if it's necessarily a good thing or a bad thing, but I just choose to not entertain it. I choose not to think about it. It's like, those things are always going to be there. And people are going to feel that way and they're going to say what they have to say. And one of the things that I would always say to myself to help me deal with those situations is, 'That's okay, because I'm going to be your boss one day.'

"That's okay, because I'm going to be your boss one day."

"And that was kind of my attitude. And that's the way I got through it and didn't let it bother me. There were definitely times when I would sit around in a meeting and somebody would say something and try to put me down or whatever, and I used to just sit there and smile because that's what I would be thinking and they had no idea. And now, it's coming to fruition because some of those people, I do manage. I get the last laugh and the last smile."

"Another thing that did help, my company sent me on a retreat for a weekend, and it was twelve women, and they had two life coaches come in, and it was three Black women in the group. We were the only three Black women in sales management [at the time] in Nike, and so, one of the leaders, a White woman, middle-aged, said, 'I just have to ask you this.' And it came out of nowhere, like left field and she said, "Do you guys feel like you have to work three times as hard to get half as far? Like has that been ingrained in you in your lifetime or in your career?' We all three kind of looked at each other like, 'I'm not answering that!' We're all taught by our parents that you have to do that. And she said, 'I'm just here to tell you that that's not true. You don't have to do that.' And we all kind of looked at each other like, 'That's not true!' We did not want to entertain it. We did not want to believe it. And I even told her, "I have to tell you, that's not true. I just don't believe it. And how can you tell me that as a White woman? You just don't know." And she kept saying it over and over again. And I thank her for saying that, because it put things in perspective for me to where I just don't care anymore. Where I used to really probably let it bother me. Now, it's like, 'Whatever.'"

Though of course, there are always legal avenues available for blatant discriminatory acts which result in differential treatment, as it relates to the more common occurrences of micro-aggressions such as the slights or dismissals of your perceptions of your own reality, as these women have shown, a good part of the battle is won or lost with how you react to the situation. Whether you choose to simply ignore disrespectful actions, knowing that in the end, you'll get the last laugh or make the decision to have courageous conversations by addressing sensitive issue frontally, the bottom line is to value yourself, value your abilities, and know that you belong..

The road to success in Corporate America for Black women is certainly far from easy. But it's far from impossible as well. When you plan your career, consistently over deliver, self-promote, assemble a stellar Career Dream Team, network like a BOSS, learn how to communicate with power and understand how to navigate the continuing reality of racism and sexism at work in a way that preserves your dignity and keeps your self-respect in-tact, you can ultimately ascend to the heights to which you aspire. These Sistahs did it and so can you.

Exceptional Black Woman Vision & Action Guide

1. The first step in developing a successful Career Plan is to start by knowing the prerequisites for success. With your ultimate goal in mind, what patterns do you see among those who have previously met with success? What skills do they possess? What experiences have they acquired? What credentials do they hold? Take a moment to list out the prerequisites you've uncovered in your research and take a moment to identify how those prerequisites compare with your background. What do you need to do to ultimately position yourself for your dream?

2. Who do you currently have on your Career Dream Team? What mentors, advocates, coaches or sponsors can you reach out to, either directly or indirectly to fill your squad? Of those individuals listed, which ones will you reach out to and share your long-term career aspirations?

3. In your personal journal, go about the process of mapping out a Career Plan. Be sure to include specific time-delineated deadlines. Feel free to solicit the support of a trusted mentor or career coach to help with this process. For help with this, you can always connect with us at www.avisjonesdeweever.com. Just remember, don't reinvent the wheel here. Do your research. And follow proven pathways to success.

CHAPTER 5

Leading Change

<CC *Dr. Height taught us when you're at the table, know that you're at the table...and be ready to play.* >>

—Melanie Campbell
President & CEO, National Coalition on
Black Civic Participation
Convener, The Black Women's Roundtable

There is something special about those who lead change. Those women who know their purpose in this world runs deeper than their own personal experience or even the span of their lifetime. Women who are the change-makers. The ones who engage in a million unseen acts that ultimately result in dynamic social, legislative, or cultural shifts which expand opportunities or improve outcomes for millions. They do the work. Often in silence, without acknowledgment, but consistently with power and effectiveness. They lead change. And in the process, they produce a better world for us all.

Many years ago, I had the privilege of working with one of this nation's most historic change-makers during the final years of her life. Upon her death, I had the honor of ascending to executive leadership of her beloved, National Council of Negro Women, taking her lessons with me along the way. Iconic Civil Rights Leader and Women's Rights Advocate, Dr. Dorothy Irene Height was more than a boss to me. She was, instead, a living, breathing, personification of courage, commitment, consistent preparation, and brilliance, all rolled up into a neatly coiffed and elegant package. A consistent force for change for most of her 98 years on this planet, she was one of those rare activists who boldly and consistently fought for both race and gender justice in the U.S. and around the world. Her work is legendary. But more importantly, it lives on.

Ascending to leadership in this particular professional realm comes with its own set of distinct challenges, often dependent upon the environment in which you seek to make your mark. If you're looking to push for change on behalf of the Black community specifically, that means in many cases, you'll have to become particularly adept at navigating perceptions of leadership being the exclusive domain of men. Likewise, if you're looking to impact change in the area of women's rights, often you'll need to push to ensure a focus on the particular needs and challenges of women of color. On the other hand, if the impact you're seeking to make is to apply to the broader context, that often means you must become masterful at ironically both inserting *and* overcoming issues of race and gender simultaneously. In all of these circumstances however, if your interests ultimately include ascending to leadership within a well-established organization, you must become adept at forming intergenerational linkages that are free from distrust or jealousy, and instead, reflect an air of mutual respect. Who said doing well was going to be easy? The only promise is, that it's worthwhile.

The Key to Making a Difference

United States Congresswoman Gwen Moore, the first African-American ever elected to Congress from the state of Wisconsin, has spent her entire life defying the odds. The eighth of nine children, she knows all too well what it's like to grow up feeling the sting of hunger as a consistent part of her daily experience. Although economically, her family struggled, intellectually, her home was bountiful. She describes her mother as brilliant, someone who coached children at her church to win oratory contests, and whom would later in life, earn her college degree and ultimately be named as one of the best poets of the English-speaking world. Perhaps it was this dual existence, of understanding from a very personal perspective the sting of poverty, while being intellectually fed at an extraordinarily level that uniquely prepared her for the role she now assumes so brilliantly. Still, had she allowed her fate to be limited to the narrow confines of what others believed was possible, she wouldn't be here. So from her perspective, the first, and most important step in making a difference, is believing that you can.

"I won my first seat in the [State] Assembly that my predecessor urged me to run for, and it's primarily, a white seat. Our current Governor, Scott Walker, ran against me in the next round. His explanation to his Republicans, who reported back to me was, 'you know, it's a white district, and I'm white.' Still, I won that, and the first [State] Senate seat I won was also a primarily white district. But I think that in running for Congress, a lot of people that would've could've should've supported me, didn't because they believed I couldn't win."

"I could tell you that I know for a fact, that had I listened to all the noise, I wouldn't be here. So, very early on, I guess the same defiance that I had as a child, enabled me to not listen to those voices that said, 'You can't do it.' Because there were plenty of people who said it can't be done, it just can't be done. People mean well. They don't want me to lose. But they just didn't believe. They did not believe that white people would rise above the color thing and elect me. That Black people could rise above their despair and turn out at better numbers than they had. They just didn't have the faith. They didn't believe, just like they didn't believe for Obama for a long time. It's hard to believe. And if you don't believe in yourself, you can't necessarily expect other people to believe either."

Believing in herself and in her ability to meet the needs of her community was not only foundational to the success of Congresswoman Moore, the same belief inspired City Councilwoman Tameika Divine, as a 29-year-old, to break political barriers in her own hometown. Frustrated by her City Council's decision not to fund a domestic violence initiative, she challenged herself to not just lament the problem, but to be part of the solution. Divine looked at the make-up of the Council and saw no one that looked like her. Though two African Americans were there, both were men, and there was no one younger than fifty who held a seat. It became clear to her that there was a need for representation far beyond that which was reflected in the current Council make-up. So despite the doubters, the diminishers, and the non-believers, she looked inward and believed in herself enough to run. In spite of the odds and significant resistance she faced, she moved forward, and perhaps to the surprise of many, challenged a fifteen-year incumbent, and came out on top.

"When I was first running, I had a lot of naysayers, some of them who were African American, because I didn't have family members who were already elected officials or had worked on political campaigns before. I had people saying why didn't I wait my turn for one of the "Black" seats? I had a lot of people telling me how difficult it would be. I had people spreading rumors about me and vandalizing my signs. I even had people sending flyers to the African American communities saying that I was a Republican and that I had deceived them. And for African Americans in the South, [Republican] was a dirty word. I didn't understand all that would be a part of it. But I had the attitude that if I didn't win, what's the worst thing that would happen? If I didn't win, I just didn't win. It wouldn't kill me. It wouldn't take away my self-esteem. It would be a learning experience. So since I wasn't afraid of losing, nothing else would hurt."

And because of her strength of conviction, fearlessness, and her unwavering commitment to try, even if the path was neither easy nor guaranteed, she pushed forward successfully, ultimately becoming the first Black woman to grace the City Council of Columbia, South Carolina. Now, thirteen years later, she still serves her city in this capacity. She's still making a difference. And she's still addressing those issues that without her, may have very well, just fallen by the wayside.

Creating change, though, can take many forms. While elected leadership remains a critical point of impact, it's far from the only one. Ours is a history steeped in the power of movement-building, organizing, and agitating as a way of disrupting the status quo such that the discomfort associated with business as usual ultimately supersedes the benefits associated with the maintenance of injustice. It is this approach to creating change that has been reinvigorated and in many ways, reinvented by the Black Lives Matter Movement. Founded and largely organized by Black women, this is a movement that has not only elevated the issue of the inappropriate use of lethal force by police departments across the nation, it is also one that has in key ways, literally redefined what it means to lead.

Inspired by the teachings of Ella Baker, a key, but often unheralded Civil Rights Icon, this new generation of leaders have made real her notions around the critical nature of diffused leadership. As a result, they've created a movement that is not defined by or limited to merely one designated and elevated "leader" but instead, one that is advance by an abundance of leaders, fighting a broad-scale battle in defense of Black lives in a variety of communities, through a multitude of ways, but all with one simple goal—"stop killing us."

According to Ifeoma (Ify) Ike, Co-Founder of Black and Brown People Vote, Director of the Young Men's Initiative for the City of New York, and activist in what she terms, the Movement for Black Lives, there are still some essential elements of "traditional" leadership that remain, even among this new generation of leaders.

"The movement that prioritizes Black lives is a leader-FULL movement. A lot of us entered into this without a name for it. Before there was a very good and timely hashtag, or before we had the social media tools to do all of this. Through my experience, leadership has been accidental. And to me, that's the beauty of it. It was the urgency of, 'Something needs to happen, and so, I'm going to do something.' But there is still a somewhat traditional aspect of leadership in that, you are not a leader, if you don't have followers. So in a lot of ways, what we're also seeing is Black trust in Black people. We're seeing Black trust in Black

youth. So while we're talking about being leader-full, I think it's important that we still elevate when people lead. We need to do a better job of actually recognizing people who actually lead and understand that there are actual leaders behind the scenes."

"So while the media will focus on the public displays of activism, whether it's Ferguson, whether it's Ohio, or New York City, what we saw is that none of those things just happened. So if all you see is a hashtag and a million people behind the hashtag, then the people behind the scenes did their job, because that's what they want you to see. But what people don't see is the hours that it took to put that together, right? They don't see the focus groups that determined that this idea is better than that idea. The ability to check each other and make sure group-think isn't happening. There are some real traditional leadership strategies, for those of us that have gone through the academia of it that organically came through."

"And there are also elders in this movement that have been in other movements. Whether that's the Amadou Diallo [case] or whether it was fighting for Sean Bell, or whether it was the anti-Apartheid movement. They were active as well. So there are leaders that in a lot of ways, have offered insight like, 'We've been here before, and this is a move to consider.' So for me, the definition is not just one definition, and why the leader-full definition of what's going on is okay with me, is that when I hear leader-full what ought to be said is it's full of others, it's full of ideas, it's full of thought, and it's not just one person's actions. And also full of the understanding that we need a whole lot of things going at one time for this to work."

Making a difference in this contemporary Movement for the Preservation of Black lives, is then, not about formal structures of leadership ascension at all. It's not about winning an election; it's not about getting a promotion or having the baton of leadership passed in any formalized way. It's all about action. It's about seeing what needs to be done, connecting with like-minded people who are also engaged in the struggle, and then adding your skills, your knowledge, your time, and your efforts to the cause you hold dear.

Or it could look like gaining insight from others active in the struggle and replicating those actions in your locality, where something too, needs to be done. So while this movement is already leader-full, there is still space to grow. There are still needs to fill. And there is still room, for yet more, to lead.

As Ify reminds us,

> *"We need more leaders. We need more people to stumble into leadership. We need more people to trust those leaders. And we need more people to provide grace, because they're also learning to lead. It requires outcomes that some of us have never seen before. And while there have been some visible, defined, leaders, and that's important for representation purposes, moving forward, I'm excited to see what new leaders will show up."*

Trust and believe—she's not the only one.

Negotiating Race in "Other" Places

Beyond the streets, and in more traditional working environments, change-making occurs through decidedly different approaches. Dr. Pauletta Walker, International President of Delta Sigma Theta Sorority, Inc., is a self-described child of the Civil Rights Movement. As such, she's faced more than her fair share of professional challenges related specifically to issues of race. But rather than shrink from these challenges, she's spent a lifetime standing up to them, taking action against them, and in each and every instance, she's come out on top.

Having successfully sued her employer for racial discrimination, she then did the unthinkable. She refused to leave the same institution that she took legal action against. Her legal case inspired others to take action of their own, ultimately leading to a change in discriminatory hiring practices at the university. For others in her situation, taking such a brave stand and then remaining in the environment that was the source of the litigated wrong, may have been a tad awkward, to say the least. But to Dr. Walker, feeling "awkward" was the furthest thing from her mind. She knew she was right. She knew change needed to happen. And she did what needed to be done to make that change occur.

"I was fine! Now, they may have felt a little awkward, but I was fine. I hadn't done anything wrong. I was very comfortable. I'm comfortable with me. And they couldn't deny that what happened had happened. It wasn't emotional. This is what happened. So afterward, they really bent over backward."

She further explains,

"I know racism when I see it. I know sexism when I see it. I recognize it. But one of the lessons that I learned is that the best way to make change is to become a part of that system. You can't be external, and not be at the table where the decisions are being made and expect change to happen, because when we sit at the table, it changes the agenda. [When] you're not even in the room, they can make all kinds of decisions, and then here you are, after the fact, trying to undo something. Had you been there, you may not have been able to stop it, but you may have derailed it, at least for a moment. So, I'm just always one that believes you need to be where you're not expected."

For Dr. Walker, becoming a part of the system was predicated on building a history of excellence. As a leader in her professional space, she earned the ability to have access to decision-making circles and once in those critically important spaces, she failed to sit by silently when questionable actions were afoot. As she described it, she played the role of inside agitator, ultimately becoming a constant force in the evolution toward greater fairness, diversity, and inclusion in her professional workspace.

"You know how sometimes, you can feel a hair on your face? You can't see it, but you can feel it. And so you find yourself just doing this (gestures feeling her face,) and no matter how much you do this, that little hair, it's like an agitator. So I tell people all the time, be the hair on the face. Just be the hair on the face. Just

agitate a little bit. Enough to where, you're going to pay me some attention, cause you're going to get tired of doing this all the time (gesturing at her face). You're going to stop and look in the mirror and say, 'What is that?'"

Now, to be clear, this propensity for agitation was not always met with acceptance and change. In fact, at times, it spurred professional foes and outright attempts at intimidation. But even in these situations, Dr. Walker failed to back down. In fact, she describes one situation in which she had a conversation with a colleague who was bold enough to issue a veiled threat her way. But in the end, it was she, who was left standing.

"I was in a conversation once with a person, and thought he was a good person, and later found out he really wasn't. Because of my position of being Chair of Black Faculty and Staff, he asked me to come to a meeting. At this meeting, he was preceding to tell me how he pretty much gets his way. He said, 'I'm sort of like a German Shepard.' I said, 'German Shepard?' He said, 'Yea, I have a big bite.' I said, 'Oh, okay. Well, I tend to be a Doberman Pincher.' He said, 'What's that?' I said, 'A Doberman Pincher will let you in the house, but you can't ever get out!' Well, when we did what we needed to do to get rid of him, at his reception, I went up to him and said, 'Woof, Woof!' I kept walking, and never looked back."

Dr. Walker's bold approach toward addressing institutionalized racism within her professional environment is not the only approach you can take or even the most advisable approach in every situation. But when you have the authority, and you find yourself at critical decision-making tables, as Dr. Height so wisely advised, *know* you're there. *Know* you have power. And don't be afraid to use it.

Heather McGhee, President of Demos, a major New York City-based progressive public policy organization, takes a somewhat different approach when faced with unfair situations that seemingly stem from issues of race. Depending upon whether the slight is personal or institution, her manner of addressing it varies from prioritizing her own sense of self, to engaging potential allies, and inviting offenders to "do better."

"My reaction is to be an iron hand in a velvet glove. Which is first to do the work myself to make sure that I'm not getting triggered and starting to undermine my own self-esteem. That's usually the first thing that happens. You get slighted in some way and then it makes you question who you are. I go there first and re-assert my own worth and the worth of all people like me. I don't believe in Black inferiority. And I don't believe in women's inferiority. I have so many images I can pull up in my mind to negate those cultural notions."

"If it's institutional, I can think of a time when I've engaged white allies. I can think of a time when I've just had a personal conversation, and I've said, 'I don't think you knew you were doing this, but I think you're better than this. And I'm going to invite you to be better than this."

"In America, everyone wants to be thought of as good. We have little institutional memory of slavery and genocide. That's something you have to contend with in social justice organizations because the people here really think that they're good. So you need to be aware of that, and if something's triggered, then you can invite people to act better."

Heather's softer approach to producing change reflects a keen understanding of her distinct context. As a Black woman leading a progressive organization made up of a predominately white staff committed to the idea of social change, she must take into consideration not only the differences in cultural experiences, but the impact of a lifetime of unseen privileges which may, at times, create situations where the offender is authentically unaware that their transgressions are actually offensive. In those instances, appealing to their base intention to "do good," while specifically pointing out the misstep and inviting better behavior in the future, creates a situation where defenses are down, you're heard, and the offender knows, that's one "mistake" that need not happen ever again.

Still, Heather understands, that ultimately, the best defense against racism, sexism, or any form of intolerance, is to acquire a firm, and deep

"The most damaging elements of racism and sexism is the way that beliefs about inferiority infect your own mind."

appreciation and understanding of your own worth. Quite matter-of-factly, she states,

> *"The most damaging elements of racism and sexism is the way that beliefs about inferiority infect your own mind. So sometimes I say to people, 'imagine what a privileged white man would say or do in this situation. Imagine what it's like to be confident in your own worth. We should all have that—the privilege of belief in our own worth."*

While this mindset—an unshakeable belief in one's own worth—may be a challenge to some, for Dr. Julianne Malveaux, it appears as effortless as breathing. Nothing less than an intellectual child prodigy, Dr. Malveaux entered Boston College after only completing the eleventh grade, and then left three years later with both a Bachelor's and a Master's Degree in hand—in economics, no less. She then went on to complete her Ph.D. at MIT. With such an impressive set of credentials, she, no doubt, had the ability to shape her career in any direction she could have imagined. But it was the love for her people, which ultimately produced a multi-faceted warrior for change.

Whether as an author, a syndicated columnist, a political commentator, university professor or President Emerita of Bennett College, Dr. Malveaux had a singular focus throughout her professional experience—the betterment of Black people. And so for her, to effectively address the multifaceted challenges faced by the Black community, it's been critical to be able to craft a career that allowed her the ability to be fluid, and to address the needs of the community in a multitude of ways. That said, for her, it's not about preparing to lead only in one specific space. Instead, it's about being prepared for them all.

"My people are my passion. Black folk are just my passion. I always tell people, it's like W.E.B. DuBois was my first husband. I'm fashioned for Black people. If you want to make a difference, you can figure out how to do it. If you want to make a living, you can figure that out too. You get yourself as trained as you can educationally to get the tools you need to do things that touch your heart and make a difference."

But despite being "fashioned for Black people," Dr. Malveaux wisely understands, that she must interface effectively across cultures to maximize the impact she produces for those she seeks to serve. She calls this ability "situational awareness."

"I watch sisters. Some people have a very soft manner and strong fist. Some have a strong manner. Situationally understanding who you are and how you might want to modify that behavior given your situation is important. I've been wearing kente cloth forever. It's my trademark. But I know better than to go to a meeting with a funder wrapped all up in kente. You know if you go to a funder meeting wrapped all up in kente, you ain't going to get the money. At some point in my life I found it important to invest in a collection of gray suits. You're never going to change who you are. Your inner is your inner. But situationally, you can adapt."

For Teresa Younger, President of the Ms. Foundation for Women, adapting often means understanding how perceptions often impact approach, when it comes to expressing ourselves in powerful, white male dominated environments. Through the years she's come to know that expressing with passion, her perspectives on issues she cares about, can often be interpreted as something very different by others. And from her perspective, those perceptions are just as likely to be driven by race, as they are to be driven by gender. She warns:

"Some of the most shocking of experiences or moments that as women of color leaders, we have to check, is when we're passionate about moving something forward; passionate about expressing our thoughts, and how that gets picked up or perceived by those around us. And how we then react to that. We have to constantly check ourselves."

"I've worked on collective bargaining [issues], and we've bought women's groups to the table because the male-dominated unions weren't getting anywhere. And I said to my staff at the time, let's get six women's organizations to the table, let's invite them to the meeting so we're not the only ones in the room, and let's push this through. The bill went all the way through. On the final night, when final negotiations were going on, there was a White male in the room, and he negotiated away a piece of the bill that was detrimental. It was really awful. He gave away the ability to take time off to care for a parent under the paid sick laws. Of course, I found out within hours. I had to pull him aside separately, where I've seen legislators and lobbyists and politicos scream at each other in the hall and I knew as many hours that I had put into this bill, I couldn't do that. I had to pull him aside. Conversations that other people get to have in public, I have to have in private, and then it becomes a he said, she said, about how the conversation really happened. But he said, 'Well, you're just over-reacting about this. You know how it goes.' He was alluding to the fact that I was a female, and I was being emotional. I said, 'No, you're being an asshole about this. We brought women to the table, and we understand that caregiving across the board is important. And you just gave that away because you didn't think about it. It's not that I'm emotional, it's that I'm passionate about this. You gave away rights that you didn't have the right to give away.'"

"I feel like you only live once. And as often as you can call the question out around race and gender, you have to do it."

Teresa understood that though she could not express publically her overwhelming disappointment in the result of those negotiations, she still had the power to directly address the issue in a very blunt way with the specific person responsible for the problem. It's an approach that ensured that her overarching perception within an institution that she still had to remain engaged in beyond this specific loss was not undermined. But it also assured, that as it relates to this specific person, he understood loud and clear that he overstepped his bounds, and ultimately, would be expected to behave differently in the future.

It's specifically because of instances like this, that it's important that we're everywhere. We need to be in the room, and particularly in Halls of Power to raise those issues others don't and fight for those things others won't.

Michele Jawando, Vice President for Legal Progress at the Center for American Progress and former General Counsel and Special Advisor to Senator Kirsten Gillibrand knows all too well what it's like to not only be one of few in the room but also to have to push constantly to expand opportunity so that others might enter. To her, the primary challenge is two-fold, the implicit if not explicitly stated belief, that one is enough. Or the belief, that you simply have to "wait your turn," even if that wait has been centuries in the making. From her perspective, the attitude she's seen time and time again can be boiled down to one simple statement, *"I hear what you're saying, but I know you, so we're okay!"*

What they don't get, in too many circumstances is that they're not okay, and neither are we. One person is not a revolution. Nor is it truly enough to change in a massive way the culture of an organization such that it will better reflect the needs of a large and growing segment of the American population. As a result, even among progressives, there remains a consistent and overwhelming tendency to protect and replicate power exclusively within White hands. So for Michele, her answer is to live up to the responsibility that comes with access to these overwhelmingly White spaces. And for her, that responsibility results in pushing to expand the hiring pool, particularly for senior positions, so as to eventually more significantly

"One person can be the beginning of expanded leadership opportunities for others."

diversify those institutions. Then knowingly watch when her colleagues are impressed with the quality of the candidates she specifically suggests. What's important to remember here is that one person *can* be the beginning of expanded leadership opportunities for others. But this scenario rarely happens on its own. You have to be willing to **push** to make it so.

Addressing Sexism in Black Spaces

One of the most enduring challenges you will face as a Black woman leader is bearing a dual identity that in most situations, takes a back seat to the "other." For example, in spaces that are designed to elevate the needs of women, it is White women's perspectives, experiences, and challenges that will be perceived as the norm and of highest priority. Likewise, in spaces that focus on race, and specifically, the Black community, issues related to the status, well-being and concerns of Black men will habitually take center-stage. It's as if Blackness is defined by "maleness" and femininity is the exclusive domain of White women.

This dynamic typically puts you at a double disadvantage, not only facing the challenge of overcoming the barriers of both race and sex within a broader culture but also, experiencing the added burden of wrestling with sexism as part of a Black cultural norm. In this context, leadership acquisition in traditionally Black environments is no less challenging than they are in largely white ones.

Roslyn Brock, Chairmen of the NAACP, devoted more than thirty years to the organization en route to her position as Board Chair. All along the way, she witnessed as men with fewer years of service under their belt and less mastery of the skills necessary for success were elevated time and time again. Still, she knew that *"delay was not denial."* With persistence and insight from a trusted mentor, she was ultimately able to pierce through to that organization's top spot, and by the way, make history in the process.

"Having grown up in the NAACP, I thought I could have achieved the role that I have now sooner than I had because I've

seen males pushed with less experience and less knowledge, but still placed in authority. When I was positioning myself to be Board Chair, I met with Dr. Height, and I asked her, 'How did you do it?' 'How in a crowded field of men, did you distinguish yourself as a woman?' And so, this is what she said to me, 'Don't worry about who gets the credit, just get the job done.' And it's hard when you know you're working day and night, and a man steps up, and he's given deference. Just get the job done?' But the truth will rise. Individuals will be an inch thick. When they can't speak to issues, then they have to step back and defer."

Not everyone, though, agrees with this approach. In fact, Baltimore Mayor Stephanie Rawlings-Blake believes that women, and especially Black women, already prefer the background. And it's not doing us any favors! We're more than willing to work hard, but that's where it ends. To get to the next level and to get there more swiftly, she believes that ultimately, "you've got to get comfortable with attaching yourself to your accomplishments." You've got to be willing to make sure others are aware of the value you bring.

Nevertheless, although Chairman Brock's route to the top may have been lengthier than it needed to be, she admits that when she finally got the nod, it was as if she made it right on time.

"I wanted to be Chair two or three years before [it happened] but it just wasn't the right time, both in my professional and personal life. And so by the time I became Chair, I was ready. And that became my campaign theme, 'Ready to Lead.' Also by that time, I was a Vice President at my job, and that helped. I'd further nurtured my relationship with the Board, and was Chair of the Centennial process. I was also talking to sponsors and telling the story of the NAACP. So it was that experience that would propel me. Now I'm the 4th woman and the youngest ever to be selected for this role."

What's critical to note here are the key boxes Roslyn checked off en route to the top spot. Although the unfairness she witnessed must have been especially frustrating, she followed Dr. Height's advice and got the job done. She excelled in her profession, further strengthening her credentials and status along the way. She also used the time to nurture relationships with other Board members, assumed key leadership opportunities, and actively demonstrated her ability to interface well with potential funders. She demonstrated, not just through her presence and loyalty, but also through her actions that she was truly ready to lead. And so ultimately, though she was young, and though she was a woman, she could no longer be denied. Still, that doesn't mean the road has been without its challenges and indignities along the way. Even now, she finds her position is often minimized, disrespected, or totally ignored altogether.

"I've been at press conferences, I've been in meetings with the President of the United States, and people always assume the man is the leader. I'm thirty years in, and I still haven't gotten my due."

Reflecting on her time as Executive Director of the National Action Network, Janaye Ingram is very open about the fact that she's witnessed sexism from a variety of standpoints within the Civil Rights community. Some blatant, and others evidenced as self-censorship among women themselves. But no matter which direction in which she noticed the tendency emanating, she made it her business to speak up and actively attempt to right the course.

"As a woman leading a national civil rights organization, our President has three jobs, so there's a lot of time when I'm in meetings with men. Sometimes there's the thought that because I'm a woman, or because I'm a young woman, I'm not going to speak up. There have been times when I have spoken up and I could see some people are surprised by that. And I continue to speak up. I'm not going to allow someone to relegate me to the corner because the men are speaking. I actually heard one of my mentees tell me that. We were planning the Trayvon [Martin] rally, and one of our staff was talking to a Chapter President about a generator.

She said to me, 'I didn't want to jump in because two men were talking.' I told her I never wanted to hear that again. I get being respectful of people, but this notion that because men are speaking you're supposed to be quiet is bull crap. You can be a man or woman, if I have something to say, I'm going to say it."

"Although I feel to some degree, Rev. Sharpton gets it, from a broader perspective, there's this notion that leadership has to be from a man and I completely reject that. I think one of the best ways to do that is by showing that you are a leader and earning the respect of those who feel like it has to be a man. When I have men come up to me and say, 'I'm impressed by your leadership,' I get the backhanded compliment. At the same time, I'm earning your respect. My presence and my leadership require that you respect it."

For Janaye, not only being a woman, but being a young woman with the charge of Executive leadership of a major national civil rights organization came with often unspoken assumptions about her ability (or perceived lack thereof). But by getting the job done and demanding respect along the way, she was able to push through pre-conceived notions around what leadership looks like, even in this, an exceedingly male-dominated space.

Melanie Campbell, President of the National Coalition on Black Civic Participation and Convener of the Black Women's Roundtable agrees that sexism within the Civil Rights community is real. However, she believes that with the new generation of leaders like Janaye and others, many of whom have distinguished themselves through the Black Lives Matter Movement, change is most assuredly afoot.

"With this generation, much of the movement is led by women. I think it's a unique time. But more investment needs to be made in Black women's leadership that's long-term and systemic. Lifting Black women's leadership and voices is needed to bring the country to a better place."

Social Justice Organizations are not the only institutions within the Black community that can be guilty of holding on to very narrow notions of leadership, often to the exclusion or at least the diminishment of women. Another such institutional powerhouse within the community is undoubtedly the Black church.

For Bishop Corletta Vaughn, Chief Apostle to Go Tell It Ministries Worldwide and cast member of the Oxygen Network's Preachers of Detroit, the call to spiritual leadership was one she felt early on in life. As a four-year-old child, she began preaching weekly sermons to eager audiences at her mom's beauty shop. All the while, it never occurred to her that there might be limits on what a girl could or should do within the confines of the church. That naiveté came to a halt on one Sunday morning she'll never forget.

> *"I was in my church. I had just been baptized, and I was ushering. I was going to bring water to the pulpit, and when I was going up, there was this old Deacon who hollered across the church, 'Corletta! You can't go up there! Women don't go up there! Girls don't go up there!' When I got home that night, my dad and my mom sat me down and told me that they were under the doctrine that women couldn't preach. It was the first time I heard that in my life. My father was very intentional about letting me know he didn't believe that, and that's not what the Bible said. So he buffered a lot of stuff from me. Kept me safe. And I just never knew I couldn't do it. I mean, what would come into a child's mind that you can't do something? Children are brave. And children, if they're in the right environment, they don't see any challenges to anything."*

With the belief that there were no limits on her capabilities, Corletta ventured beyond her father's protective space and formally answered the call to ministry in 1974. About a decade later she would meet an Apostle that would change her life. As she sees it, he recognized her gift, and so he took her under his wing, trained her, and set her along the path of leadership that she occupies today. Still, after dedicating over four decades to her calling, Bishop Vaughn continues to find herself amazed at the deeply-held negative notions around women's leadership held by some within an institution that ironically, is overwhelmingly maintained through the consistent support—financial and otherwise—of women.

"One of the greatest mistakes I ever made was just not being familiar with the prejudice and marginalization of women that is prevalent in the church. I approached everything with a bit of naiveté; bright-eyed, bushy-tailed. Looking back now, I see it. But it made me better prepared. It forced me to go to school. It forced me to study. It forced me to have conversations with people. It was a great mistake, made good. Still, I don't understand the deep hatred that people have about women pastors. It's not the doctrine; it's hatred."

For Bishop Vaughn, her father's protective reflex along with her own prolonged naiveté shielded her to some degree from the negative backlash that sometimes occurs around issues of women's leadership roles, particularly as it relates to the ministry. Apparently sensing the need to prove her legitimacy, she invested the time and effort necessary to become exceedingly prepared to master what it is she believes she was called to do. For her, whatever resistance she faced along the path, ultimately, did nothing but make her better.

Similarly, Presidential Advisor, Pastor, and the United States Ambassador-at-Large for International Religious Freedom, Dr. Suzan Johnson Cook relied on a commitment to excellence, exceeding intellectual and spiritual preparation as well as a strong sense of self to ultimately break barriers over and over again throughout her career.

In 1983, she became the first women to become a Senior Pastor in the 200-year history of the American Baptist Churches. She also became the first and only woman to hold the position of the official Chaplain of the New York City Police Department, a post she held for over twenty years. Along the way, she founded the Bronx Christian Fellowship Baptist Church and was subsequently elected as President of the Hampton University Ministers' Conference, a conference which represents all of the historically African-American denominations. But her consistent path-breaking ways don't mean that early on she failed to face resistance. She did. However, a well-respected ally addressed that resistance frontally, and in so doing, cleared the path for her brilliance to shine.

"I went into the Christian ministry, not knowing I was making history, but I became the first Black female pastor in the 200-year history of the American Baptist Churches. And I didn't know I was the first, I just knew I was called, and I was talented. And then the late, Gardner Taylor, stood with me, and he was maybe about 75 at the time. He was called the Dean of Preachers, and there was this buzz that maybe women weren't called to preach. Dr. Gardner Taylor came over and brought like 300 people from his church, and he stood with me. His presence ended the conversation. When Dr. Gardner Taylor showed up, it was like, you'd better get on board! It ended the discussion."

Both of these examples demonstrate that tearing down traditions of gender exclusion not only requires personal excellence, but it also requires, at least one well-respected ally who is willing to crack open the door. Strong relationships, undeniable ability, and earned respect can ultimately result in that one critical supporter who makes all the difference and creates the breathing room you need to make the difference you knew you were capable of, all along.

Lessons on Lifting as We Climb

If your greatest aspiration is to become a leader in a capacity that creates change, you must clearly understand that making a difference is not enough if the difference you make is static; a mere blip on a historic screen. Great leadership leads to lasting change. And the only way to ensure an impact that lingers is to make sure your work lives beyond you; that it supersedes any specific lifetime and is carried on by future generations. Understanding then, how to grow, replicate, and advance power is the true definition of effective leadership. In other words, as you're making your way to the top, all along the way, let down the ladder, and help the next Sistah with her climb.

Helping others is a responsibility Ambassador Cook has taken seriously throughout her career. Though she's achieved several firsts along her ground-breaking journey, she's been even more intentional about making sure that though she may be the first, she's never the last.

"I'm a trailblazing woman. For me, it wasn't important to make history, but it was important for me to be the first of many. So each church I left, I left a woman in charge. I set people up so that people can have leadership roles. Succession planning is very important. When you replicate, you go further. The next generation is supposed to go further than we did. It gives me a feeling of joy instead of competitiveness."

"I don't know if it's insecurity. I'm not sure of all of the factors, but it saddens me when I see people try to close a door and build a wall, rather than lift others up. Bishop TD Jakes once said that God gives talent, but man or woman gives opportunity. You have to give opportunity. Both congregations that I left, I had many women in many roles, they were visible, they were not subservient. Their gifts and their voices were amplified. Everyone who is a leader gets a signal when it's time. You give opportunities. Once there were seven women in my pulpit. People were shocked! But if there were seven men in the pulpit, no one would have spoken about it. I got the congregation to allow them to be in several leadership roles, and we raised money so they could all go to seminary."

Clearly, Ambassador Cook understands the critical nature of actively working to put in place a pipeline for the next generation of leaders. And she has made this belief an active part of who she is and what she does consistently as a leader. Spotting potential, nurturing it, providing opportunities for ascension, and then even financially investing in that potential such that it has the solid foundation necessary for it to take root and thrive is the formula she's used to ensure the change her presence created is indeed, everlasting.

Likewise, Melanie Campbell believes that the commitment to bringing others along, is in fact, an essential element of effective leadership. She knows, first hand, how essential the practice is because it was this tendency that ultimately cleared the way for her long-term success. Brought in as the Interim Executive Director of the historic organization she now leads, initially her ascension to a more permanent placement was threatened when it became common knowledge that despite her stellar performance, a man was being positioned as her replacement. But when key, well-respected leading women learned of those efforts, they addressed the issue frontally with their male peers, thereby ensuring that Melanie was not unfairly ousted. Today, twenty years later, she remains atop that bold and highly effective organization. From that experience, she learned the following:

"Dr. Height taught us this, if you're at the table, know you're at the table and be ready to play. And when you're at the table, who are you bringing? It's not just when you get in the door, you close it. What makes me excited is I see we can elevate Black women's leadership. I know we can get much further if we work together. But we have to be able to work through bad moments. Everybody your color ain't your kind, and everybody your kind ain't your color; that's real. But the power of Black women and our determination, motivated me and taught me the importance of looking out for each other. That was important to me early on in my career, and I've been able to learn from that."

Dr. Barbara Williams-Skinner, President of the Skinner Leadership Institute and Co-Chair of the National African American Clergy Network understands that despite the need for and wisdom of actively engaging and clearing a path for the next generation of leaders, there remains a real challenge with putting into practice the act of nurturing intergenerational leadership in a broad and systemic way. At the end of the day, it all boils down to one simple fact. It is the responsibility of those further along their leadership journey, to extend to others the same courtesy they received years before. And unfortunately, in far too many cases, this is a responsibility that remains unmet.

"Women are smarter than we're acting. Veteran women like myself, it's our responsibility to teach young women that [racism and sexism] is navigate-able. It's on our watch. Our generation disconnected

ourselves from the younger generation. I was the beneficiary of women like Barbara Jordan and Shirley Chisholm and people like that. They guided me. They didn't call it mentoring, but they took me under their wing. And I feel like women fifty and older need to take seriously how we got here and take every opportunity that we can to take younger women under our wing."

Facing the Enemy Within

In spite of the critical imperative to replicate our success by putting in place practices specifically meant to develop, guide, and nurture the next generation of leaders, the reality is, for far too many, this need goes unmet. This is perhaps the cruelest reality of them all. It is the realization that comes when you determine that some of the biggest roadblocks you will face, are those obstructions created and erected by someone who looks like you. Even within an arena specifically focused on producing positive change, there's no escaping this reality. Ageism, colorism, cliquishness, or a strong and unwavering desire to be "the only one," remains all too common and in many ways, continues to hold back our collective advancement.Michele McNeal-Emery, National President of 100 Black Women of America believes it is this unfortunate reality that creates an added layer of challenges for Black women who lead. In fact, from her perspective, at times, it can be those who are closest to you that can cause the deepest harm.

"Sometimes we don't like to see each other succeed. That's why as a leader, you have to be strong. Because sometimes, not everyone is going to be supportive of you. We're jealous of one another. We suffer from the crab syndrome. We do it at every age level. I've seen peers do it. People who don't want to see you get above where they are. There are some people who believe that if one of their core set of friends succeed then they succeed. You can't take all your friends with you all the time. Some of them will be very envious of what you have, because they believe since you have it, it belongs to them as well. It's like a see-saw, they'll try their best to pull you down if they see you getting too high."

See-saw tendencies or not, Natalie Cofield, Founder of Walker's Legacy, has experienced her fair share of hurts, precisely from the women she would have otherwise expected to support her the most.

"To be honest, the most difficult experiences I've had in my career have been led by African American women who've tried to sabotage me. My life experience is it's been Black women. It's been a colorist thing, classism thing, ageism thing. Sometimes people see me as this light skinned privileged Black woman, but they don't know me. They don't know my story. They don't know all my clothes during my freshmen year came from the Salvation Army, or that I worked three jobs in High School. Just 'cause you have a degree, doesn't mean you're a millionaire."

The sad reality is, competitiveness, pettiness, and jealousy is real. But beyond the personal attacks and superficial judgements, Barbara Perkins, President of the International Black Women's Public Policy Institute points out that one of the most consistent challenges she's witnessed throughout her own career, and one that she continues to see is the issue of ageism and the degree to which some Black women habitually and intentionally hold young women back.

"Ageism was a big problem for me, and still is—the way we minimize the contributions that younger women bring. You know you have a voice. You know you're willing. You know you have preparation. But you have to wait for the green light to get in the mix or voice your opinion. And that's ageism within our community. We minimize the contributions of young women. We stifle them in so many ways. Their views are not valued. Almost every place I go, I remind them that it's not okay to just invite young people in the room and not listen to them. We run out of time, or we minimize them, or, 'They're just young people' as opposed to really valuing what they bring."

It's this diminishment that Stefanie Brown-James, Founder of Brown Girls Lead and Co-Founder of Vestige Strategies has felt the sting of, time and time again. For her, it's a reality that's all too commonplace,

> *"I've experienced a lot of woman-to-woman sexism. Part of it is ageism. Women who like to be the only ones in the room. Women who feel threatened by another sister coming up. Where there should be a partnership, there seems to be competition."*

For other women, the problem may not be ageism per se, but being on the receiving end of a lack in some women's faith in leadership as advanced specifically by other women. It's as if some women believe that true leadership, not only often is, but frankly, should always be the exclusive domain of men. From Bishop Vaughn's perspective, it all stems from a consistent yet irrational fear that some women have regarding their own.

> *"What has been given to most women is a fear of women. That's one of the things we need to address. I hear women say all the time, I don't trust women. I hear women say, I would never go to a church where a woman is a pastor. So we give language that is self-sabotaging, it sounds like you're talking about another woman, but when you're talking about another woman, you're talking about yourself. We have to come to the point of self-worth."*

Roslyn Brock most assuredly agrees when she soberly states:

> *"We look at the enemy, and it is us because we will not give a sister the same opportunities that we will a man. There is no way I would be where I am if I didn't have powerful mentors, men, and women, who kept me grounded and kept me moving forward. But for the woman issue, we really need to grapple with that if we are to be successful. As women, often, we want, what we won't give."*

It's precisely this type of toxicity that potentially dooms our chance at long-term, broad-scale advancement. Hoarded power, is fleeting power. It's power with an expiration date. It's merely a spark in a dark night that will never eventually evolve into a bright new day. Until we, collectively, as Black women, move past the tendency of some to hold on, with clenched fists, to what small sliver of power that may come our way, our ability as a collective, will forever be stunted; never moving beyond a mere fragment of all it is capable of becoming.

The million-dollar question is, how do you overcome all of those obstacles? How do you properly navigate all the pitfalls placed in your way both by outsiders and in some instances, by those who look just like you? The answer, as Dr. Malveaux wisely shared, is that you just "manage it." Much like a diabetic "manages" their disease, you must learn to push through those negative encounters and hurtful incidents as a part of the normal course of how you live your life. Of course, there are a multitude of weapons at your disposal that you can use to make this task of managing unfairness a bit easier. Like Dr. Walker, you may choose to use the tool of litigation and seek legal recourse for particularly egregious discriminatory acts that you face along your path. In other circumstances, like Heather McGhee, it may be more practical and effective to have direct conversations with those who at least perceive themselves as fundamentally good, and then challenge them to do better. You can also form alliances with well-respected insiders who can crack open the door of opportunity and in so doing, verify your legitimacy to others. Or you can just engage in the work, knowing that you are one of many leading change without waiting for any official green light to start along that path.

Whichever you choose, know this. Your biggest and most powerful weapon in each of these circumstances comes by way of fully embracing who you are, being comfortable in your own skin, and becoming intimately aware of your own capabilities.

Know too that sometimes, this awareness will require that you go your own way. It may necessitate that you build something new, something uniquely your own, and something that meets a need heretofore inadequately addressed or perhaps, not addressed at all. Sometimes in life, you must be bold enough to create your own space to shine.

Exceptional Black Woman Vision & Action Guide

1. In what ways do you want to lead change and why?

2. Who are the natural allies in your space who you can gain insight from and can help crack open the door for your ascension to the next level? What will you do now to grow or nurture those relationships?

3. What activities can you engage in to either strengthen your skillset or increase the impact of the contributions you're currently making within your organization? In other words, how can you best demonstrate your effectiveness and readiness to lead?

CHAPTER 6

Successful Sistahpreneurship

*** Understand that there will always be challenges. There will always be roadblocks, fear,
whatever it is. I believe these challenges are put
in front of you to see how much you're ready to
sacrifice. How much you'll push to get to where
you want to be. They're just tests to see if you
really want this. ***

—Gabrielle Jordan
Teen Entrepreneur, Author, and Philanthropist
Award Winner, Black Girls Rock!

For many years before I actually took the plunge, I longed to
be an entrepreneur. Inspired by my father's amazing journey
from sharecropper to successful businessman, I craved a future
that would one day lead to entrepreneurial success. Although this
aspiration existed, I had exactly zero clues on how to get there. For
years I stayed stuck; encapsulated in the self-imposed boundaries of
a meaningful career, one that I enjoyed, but still one that resulted
in the perpetual motion of building someone else's dream, while
putting off my own.

Over the years, I'd seen others make the shift. And I watched
in awe as they successfully transitioned from employee to entrepreneur. However, the details of exactly how they made the move were
seemingly shrouded in mystery. I wondered, "What's their secret?"
"How'd they do it?" And most importantly, "Can I do it too?"

123

When I finally decided to take the plunge, I did so thoughtfully and with the commitment to learn as much as I could to maximize my chance of success. Now, as I stand on the other side of that dream, the owner of not one, but two successful businesses, I constantly meet others who find themselves at the same place I found myself only a few years ago; wondering, how I did it and if they can too? The answer to that question is a resounding, YES! With vision, commitment, and a sound plan of action, anything is possible. So if in your chest beats the heart of an entrepreneur, craving to create something you can one day call your own, then know that it's possible to live your dream. But it all starts with the simplest of notions. Make the commitment to first and foremost, do what you love.

Do What You Love

Huffington Post Live Host, freelance journalist, and political commentator, Zerlina Maxwell loves what she does. She spent years creating a career that freed her from the typical post-law school experience. Making a living in front of cameras instead of inside courtrooms, didn't come with a roadmap. Instead, through personal development, along with the discipline of goal-setting and strategic action, she pieced together the puzzle of a new path that created the reality she wanted all along. And the best news is, so can you.

"I'm doing what I would do even if I weren't paid. I'm doing work that doesn't feel like work. I think a lot of people think that's impossible, but the economy has forced more entrepreneurs. Goal setting is big for me. Writing it all down--three months, six months, a year [goal targets]. I think self-help got a bad rap at some point, I don't know why, but personal development is super important. You have the internet. You have an audio book you can throw on your iPad, iPod, your iPhone, and you can potentially improve. If you procrastinate too much, you can figure out how to not do that. If you want a certain business, you can find information on that. [You] might say, I want to get an article in the Nation, but then don't go through the steps to get it done. That's the work. The

people that are successful—yes there are structural reasons, they may have more money and families with access, that's true—however it's also true that you can wake up in the morning, write out a to-do list, and take steps to work toward your goal."

"So for me, it's about having a plan, writing it down, and being as specific as possible. The brainstorming that I do when I think about the next big goal, I write bullet points and then minutia details. I didn't just wake up one day and end up on MSNBC. I woke up one day and said, hey I want to get on TV. How do you get on TV? Well, okay now Google people on TV. Now, do people on TV write for certain websites? Do people on TV get media training? What kind of segments do they do? I went from that thing everyone does, 'I wish I could do this,' 'I wish I could do that,' to 'Here's a plan that I wrote out and it's done.' You do get your breaks here and there, but most of the time it's because you have a plan in place, and you were already moving towards your goal. You had a plan in place, and you were moving that way. You had momentum."

As Zerlina accurately points out, momentum is impossible to acquire without prior action. It's easy to fall in love with an idea for a business that leverages your strengths, natural talents, and doesn't feel like "work," but wishing it to be so is not enough. Determine what's required. Develop a plan to get there, and commit to the daily actions that are necessary to ultimately create the business and lifestyle of your dreams.

Medical Doctor, Best-Selling Author, and Health, Fitness, and Beauty Guru, Dr. Phoenyx Austin has defied convention for what one typically does with a medical degree. Instead of spending marathon hours in emergency rooms or building a practice juggling hundreds of patients, she has woven her love of literature and science into entrepreneurial pursuits that have allowed her to inform thousands on how to live healthier, happier lives. The idea first struck her when she was still in medical school after coming face to face with a particularly disturbing case.

"I had a patient one day, and I could smell the stench of dying flesh. She called it a small cut, but I knew it was necrotic tissue.

*I had her remove her shoe. Her foot was totally black and completely
numb. We had to admit her to the hospital that day to have her foot
amputated. I wrote about her and sent it to the local newspaper. I
wrote it in a story format and it caught the eye of a producer at Fox.
He thought it was a physician who wrote the story. He had me on to
do a segment on healthy living. Then I started watching people like
Dr. Oz and I realized there were things I could do to give advice on
a massive scale. I could impact not only one person at a time; I could
literally touch thousands, if not millions at one time."*

With that epiphany, even as a medical student, her focus changed.
She began to see a very different path for her professional future
than would be the case for most of her classmates. For Dr. Phoenyx,
the choice was clear. She would become a non-practicing physician;
one who could effect change on a much larger scale by informing
potentially millions on issues of healthy living through multi-media
engagement and her distinct writing style. Although her vision was
clear, for others, it was quite a bit more difficult to see.

*"I didn't have any fear. My parents, other doctors, and other peo-
ple were terrified. But I just got this idea in my head and really
didn't fear it. I've always been the type where I get this idea in
my head, and I don't have fear. I just know what I want and
know that I have to take certain steps to get it. And that's fine
because ultimately that's what I want to do...Now I write and
publish books. My books have gone on to be best sellers. I'm a
non-practicing physician who also consults, and I love it."*

Herein lies the secret that those who have been bold enough
to pursue their business dreams come to realize. Your vision is *your*
vision. Not everyone will see it. Not everyone will understand it.
And not everyone will even believe that it's possible. But you must
refuse to bend to their limited perceptions of your capabilities. Instead, hold on to your vision, despite the naysayers and even in the
face of their fears, doubts, and objections. Now, of course, do your
research. Develop a plan and assess for yourself the viability of your

aspirations. But if you've determined that what you desire is indeed possible, protect your dream. Breathe life into it. And don't allow the skepticism of others to dim what you clearly see.

For Dr. Phoenyx, the answer is simple,

"Whatever you're trying to accomplish, just do it from a place of, what do I love? Be as genuine as you can be to yourself and your desires, and you're going to be able to make the choices and walk the path that you want to walk. Just ignore what everybody else is saying and follow your heart. Every single person that I've encountered that I consider a mentor and people that I've looked at who've accomplished great things, it's consistent across the board. Whether this person is a Ph.D. or MD-level or a high school dropout, they've always followed what they loved to do, and they were ultimately, successful because of it. So, do what you love. That's governed every single choice that I've made and because of that, I've never been confused about what I need to do."

"We all know what we love to do, but it's fear that delays the whole process. You may feel like you're totally in a place where you don't know what choice you should make. It's not confusion; it's fear that's holding you back."

For Valerie Roseborough, it was the jarring experience of facing what easily could have been the most frightening time in her life that served as the inspiration to move forward with her entrepreneurial dream, rather than continuing to put it off.

A graduate of the world-renowned, Fashion Institute of Technology and having spent over two decades traveling the world as part of New York's high-powered fashion industry, the repercussions of globalization along with the tragedy of 9/11 ultimately landed Valerie in a new city, a new professional environment, and unfortunately, in one that was much less than a perfect professional fit. As challenging as these changes alone were, things quickly got even worse. Just four years after losing her mother to breast cancer, in January of 2012, Valerie got the grim news that the disease had now come for her too. Like her mother, she chose to fight it aggressively, opting for a bilateral radical mastectomy. As she bravely faced what very well could have been the lowest moments in her life, instead of sinking into despair, out of this crisis spawned a new beginning.

"During that time, as some sort of mechanism to escape and focus, The Tailored Nest [a multi-cultural lifestyle brand] came into full view. I was in a hair salon one day, and I saw a full page ad for a Fabric Mill, in Essence, magazine. When I looked in the margin, I saw it was a supplier near [me]. I went to visit the warehouse and immediately knew what the Tailored Nest would be. I told [my employer at the time] what I was going through physically. They made promises to be supportive, but they ended up terminating me half way through my cancer treatments. I had two more surgeries to go, and I couldn't stop. I felt that I had to move forward and put it all in my rearview mirror. The Tailored Nest would do that for me. That was where my head was at. It's what inspired and moti-vated me to get through what I was going through."

"What I learned from that experience is that when you put that much of yourself into something, it resonates. First people were looking at me cross-eyed. 'Do you need help?' 'Do you know what's going on?' Soon they saw that the medical side was under control. It's the psychological part of it that I think is where so many women can have difficulty. Drawing from my childhood, I knew I had to entertain myself. I had to motivate myself. And I had to figure out how I was going to make a living."

"So the collection was born two weeks after one of my major reconstructive surgeries. The photoshoot was on-sight in Vien-na—woodsy, a beautiful home. It was a big production. I styled the entire thing. It required wheelbarrows, climbing trees, and the like, but we got through it. The photoshoot allowed us to put the brochure together and put the website together. By January, I did my first show in New York, and buyers were open to it."

Out of the combination of a health crisis and the closing of a professional door, Valerie's aspiration to build a business around culturally inspired home furnishings and accessories was born. Precisely at the moment in which most would believe such a drastic step would have been impossible, Valerie used her crisis as motivation to make real a dream she'd nurtured for years. In an almost cathartic way, her treatment gave her the space to really focus on how to take this dream out of the realm of imagination and begin to put the pieces together in such a way as to ultimately grow it into a thriving business. And while it hasn't always been easy, the lesson she learned from this process is clear:

> *"It has to be authentically you. It can't be somebody else's gift or talent. It has to really be what it is you do well. What brings you the most joy? Sometimes that's masked over by life. It gets masked over by all the tasks that you have to perform. I've always said, there's nothing special about me. I was never the smartest or the prettiest kid. There was nothing special. But I just honed in until I got it right. You don't have to be perfect. You don't have to be the best. But you've got to do it. You've got to just go for it. Now the business side of things can be challenging, especially when you're a small business. But at the end of the day, I get to come home to my design studio. I still walk in the door, and love it."*

Fill a Need

For Freelance Lifestyle Journalist, Brand Consultant, and Digital Media Powerhouse, Aniesia Williams, her path to entrepreneurship was carved by neither crisis, epiphany, nor long-term aspirations. Instead, she stepped, somewhat reluctantly, onto a path that appeared before her as a result of quite effectively answering a need.

As she explains,

> *"I didn't wake up one day and say, hey, I'm going to go into business for myself. It all started when I was helping a friend out. She was about to go on this reality show, and her bio didn't look right, so I fixed it. And after I fixed hers, other people were like, 'Hey, well can you do mine?' and I was like, 'Yea, I'll do it.' And so I*

started doing folks and then they started getting expectations and started requesting and requiring things. So I was like, wait a minute now. Since you guys are requesting something, then maybe I should start charging something. I didn't know what I should charge, because I just started by helping somebody. So I started experimenting. I didn't know it, but I was undercharging. People were mad at me who were in the profession because they thought I was intentionally undercharging; I just didn't know. But when I get serious about something, I do it all out, to the best of my abilities. I go hard or go home. So I started researching things. I started going to trade shows, working conferences, and I did all this stuff. Now, I'm a smart cookie; I have an MBA. So then I started to figure it out, and I started getting really good at it. I figure out what I liked about it and what I didn't, what I wanted to do and what I didn't want to do. You have to do that. You have to figure out what works best for you."

Once she figured out "what worked best," Aniesia ran with it. Building a business that boasts a top-tier client roster including everything from some of the world's largest brands, such as Ford, Samsung, Shell and Lionsgate, to even working with the Clinton's Global Initiative and serving as the National Director for Branding, Marketing & Communications for Black Women for Obama. But it all started from being keenly aware of a need, understanding how her talents and natural abilities best filled a pre-existing niche, and then dedicating herself to learning what she had to know to be counted among the best.

For Deborah Owens, America's Wealth Coach and CEO of Owen's Media Group, a transition from Corporate America to a business of her own, was ultimately based on the desire to acquire a better handle on that illusive work/life "balance" to which so many aspire, but few ever actually accomplish. Even with that as her goal, leaving a stunningly successful career was not easy. She'd distinguished herself quickly at a major financial institution by skyrocketing up the ranks of Fidelity Investments. In only seven years' time, she'd gone from Receptionist to Vice President and along the way noticed that to her, at least, really understanding money was not quite as complex as most people thought. As such, she discovered a natural proclivity for being able to explain financial complexities in lay-persons terms. And while she knew this gift could be applied to a business of her own, her transition was gradual and devised in such a way as to leverage relationships she'd developed all along her corporate journey.

Even while still in her corporate role, Deborah developed and hosted a talk show of which, her employer was a sponsor. And by the time she was ready to strike it out on her own, guess who was one of her first clients? Her advice is simple,

> *"Don't quit your day job until you determine what relationships you have that can help you develop revenue. Don't close any doors. Don't burn any bridges. Ideally, they can be your first client."*

Over time, though, the customer-base of her business shifted, moving from organizations to individuals. The switch came at a critical time. She'd just ramped up staffing in preparation for a major contract that fell through at the last minute. It's at that moment she discovered an even greater need could be found in servicing clients directly instead of conducting training on behalf of major organizations. This shift allowed her business to grow in new directions and ultimately scaled up her work to levels unforeseen. What she learned from this process is a lesson that applies to every business owner. Listen to your customers. Discover and address their needs.

> *"It's not always about what you're selling. It's about solving a problem that's in the marketplace right now."*

Know that Excellence Breeds Longevity

Cheryl McKissack, President & CEO of McKissack & McKissack, the oldest women/people of color-owned professional design, and construction firm in the nation, knows a little something about longevity in business. Today she leads a family-owned firm that was formally incorporated in 1905, but whose roots go back much further. Even the shackles of slavery couldn't stop the entrepreneurial inclinations of this extraordinary clan. According to her genealogical research, her earliest ancestor on these shores learned the trade of brick-making and used that skill to start a business, even as a slave. This was the root of an architectural dynasty that lasts to this day. One of his sons, Gabriel McKissack, was a master carpenter and was well known for building spectacular spiral staircases. He eventually partnered with his brother, Calvin, and together, they incorporated the business in 1905. When licensing laws came into effect that threatened the future of their business, the two were barred from sitting for the required test because they were Black. Still, they didn't give up. Instead, they lobbied the Licensing Board and got one member to allow them to take the test, under the belief that they wouldn't pass anyway. But given the chance, they proved him wrong. As a result, the two became the first Black licensed architects in the nation. As the first, they received national attention. This allowed them to expand and ultimately gain licenses in a total of twenty-two states. With this as their foundation, the work of the firm exploded. They built numerous churches and Black colleges. They even built the Tuskegee Air Force Base, earning a $6.5 million government contract, the largest ever awarded to an African American at that time. Their work even expanded beyond America's borders, allowing the team to make their mark internationally.

Eventually, the company passed down to Cheryl's father. But when he became ill, her mother stepped in and brought Cheryl and her sisters into the business. Today Cheryl runs their New York City offices, her twin sister opened a branch in Washington DC and their other sister serves as an interior designer, truly keeping the business all in the family. Over the years, the McKissack & McKissack brand has continued to be a barometer of excellence. Additional branches can be found in Philadelphia, Chicago, Los Angeles and even as far away as Saudi Arabia. Their penchant for excellence continues. They've constructed numerous amazing structures including everything from university buildings on college campuses across the nation to mass transit systems, and even including the iconic Dr. Martin Luther King, Jr. Memorial as well as the Smithsonian Museum for African

American History and Culture. Theirs is a legacy of excellence. And it's this excellence that has provided an unparalleled historical foundation that has kept the business strong generation, after generation, after generation.

For Cheryl, this history of achievement is nothing short of breathtaking, but it still created for her, a special set of challenges to not only keep the legacy alive but to help it grow in the modern age and amid new surroundings.

"If you read the statistics, it's incredible that a business makes it to a second generation because usually the children don't value the business that the Founder created. It's something good that my family did. I think it's because they made us go out into the world. That changed my perspective. I didn't feel like I was just given something. I had to go out and prove who I was in my profession. And I understood that working for someone is one dynamic, but it's completely different from owning your own. And when it's not a start-up, it's a company that's been around for a while, you have a platform. You have something that sells. And you have a portfolio. And so, for me, that was a blessing. So the work comes from taking a portfolio from Nashville (their hometown and where the roots of the company were planted) and taking it to New York. That's where I had to bring my own personal creativity, fortitude, and all that to the table. New York is not a kind place. You don't just drop everything and come here and start doing stuff and find it to be easy. It's not easy. Especially in construction. Construction is definitely a good-ole-boys network. And people in this business, the good-ole-boys, they know that it builds wealth, and they want to keep it to themselves. They don't want to share the pie. So the legacy part is important, because it gave me something as an entrepreneur, to have a leg up on the beginning of a business, but I still had to bring it to the most vibrant city in the world and translate a Southern experience into a Northeastern one."

And that she did, as is a family tradition, with uncommon excellence. But even for businesses with more recent roots, it is an exceptional performance that at the end of the day, is foundational for continued success. Aneisia Williams, for example, may have started her company when friends needed her help, but she grew her company based on the level of quality that she brings to what she does. Although she develops entire marketing campaigns for the clients she serves, ironically, she's never quite needed to create one to grow her own business.

"For me, it was about word of mouth. I would literally meet people while I was doing a job. I didn't have to market my services. I would be speaking at a panel somewhere, or they would see something that I did, and they would hit me and say, can you do that for me too? I've never had to market in ten years."

Shay Wood, President & CEO of 5001 Flavors and Owner of Harlem Haberdashery, started a business with her future husband while in college. The empire they've built over the years has grown to be so beloved by their celebrity clientele, that they've not only serviced them but now also service the children of that same clientele; building, in essence, a multi-generational client roster.

As Shay describes,

"Early in the 1990's when Puffy was an intern, we started working with the early artists. We worked with Heavy D., Biggie, and a young Mary J. Blige. When Puffy started Bad Boy, we went with him. From there, we were referred by photographers and managers. By the time I graduated [college] in 1994, the business was really established. We had 100 clients and a lot of the artists we worked with had begun to start their own labels. We often took clients from obscurity to fame. We'd work with them while they'd rise and grow. We might get an unsigned artist, and in the next two years, he's in plays and movies. We grow as they grow. Red carpet appearances, their moms, their wives, their kids. Now we have a second generation of clients. We're doing Puffy's children."

Clearly, starting a business is not enough. You can love what you do, you can fill a pre-existing need in the marketplace, but if you don't do it well, your days in business are numbered. Excellence is the key to not only having a business, but *growing* a business; and building it in such a way as to maximize the chance of success for many years to come.

Network for Business Expansion

As is the case in every professional realm, for the entrepreneur especially, networks are a foundational component of success. But in this context, it's critical never to lose sight of the fact that the goal at the end of your networking rainbow is ultimately, a closed deal.

Toya Powell, Founder of Bid Compliance Solutions, a global management consulting firm, and former Vice President of the U.S. Black Chambers emphasizes the importance of being purposeful in your networking tactics. For example, instead of going to networking events only to leave with a boat-load of business cards, think strategically about what partnerships you can develop, what connections you can solidify, and above all else, don't limit yourself to just those who look like you if you really want to get ahead.

"I go to so many networking events and people are all about getting business cards. OK, what are you going to do with that card? Partnerships are critical, and being able to connect across ethnicity is key. Honestly, White men have been in this game longer than we have. They have networks and Rolodexes and such that we don't have. It's okay to work with them. It's okay to say, will you work with me? It's really about diversification. We have to know the market, and how to engage the market. Often, we need to be the first one showing up at certain events, and the last one leaving. If we show up late or if we're not making the most of each situation, then it's really putting us behind the curve. We need to be in more speaking roles. We need to ask, do you need a speaker for that event? And above all else, when the opportunity presents itself, ask for the business. Sometimes we do the meeting, but we never ask for the money, and the business never gets closed."

While closing a deal or making a sale should always be in the back of your mind, remember that sometimes business can come from the most unexpected of sources. Don't overlook those relationships you currently have that may ultimately lead to new and exciting opportunities. And when those opportunities present themselves, it's critical to be ready, willing, and able to act.

One of Cheryl's most lucrative projects came from a relationship nurtured outside of the traditional business realm altogether. Instead, it came as an unexpected opportunity landed through her charity work. As she explains:

"A woman had been reaching out to me for four years with a non-profit organization she was putting together. She decides she wants to have a Board meeting at my office, so she pulls together this group, and I meet this woman from Pegasus, which is a huge venture capitalist group, in the billions. In the meeting, she says, Cheryl, I have some friends who are trying to do some work in Saudi Arabia, they need some stadiums, would that be something you'd be interested in? Well, because I'm in sales I said, sure, and didn't think anything of it. She said great, send me your brochure, which I did. Within 24 hours, I was on a conference call with several consultants, one from France, one from Qatar, her father who was an emissary for Africa and I'm thinking to myself, 'This will never happen.' Next thing I know, I'm on a plane to London, and I'm meeting with the head of the largest construction company in Saudi Arabia. They're building eleven stadiums, and they're looking for an American firm to partner. I've now been over there several times, and we're talking a huge contract. And all this came from charity."

Remember, opportunity is everywhere. So nurturing relationships across the spectrum, even in the most unusual of spaces, is a critical component of maximizing your potential for entrepreneurial success.

Break Through the Myth of Inferiority

A primary reason why developing and nurturing relationships is key is because without them, as an unknown entity, you are especially likely to face the stubborn, but often unspoken reality of perceived inferiority. As Dr. Maya Rockeymoore, founding President and CEO of Global Policy Solutions explains, this is a situation that more often than not, must be actively disproven rather than merely passively overcome.

"The issue of Blackness is that people assume inferiority. White people tend to have a perception that you must come from a situation of extreme disadvantage so whatever you do must not be of quality. So stepping into a room and having that be the assumption, Black people have always known that you have to work twice as hard. For Black women, you have to work three times as hard. Whenever I face that, it comes out, and it comes out early. It used to get my hackles early on. But now, I understand it's not about me, it's about them."

Still, to address the issue, she encourages an approach that takes into consideration the very real, even if unfair, issue of perception.

"Men are considered leaders and women are considered aggressive, or worse, B's. I've learned you have to modulate your tone. You have to have a steady and consistent presence. You can't show emotion in the way a man can. You have to modulate your behavior. Everything from your tone to your body language in order to manage perception. There was one point in my life when I was like, I'm going to be who I'm going to be. They have to deal with it. Now I've come to terms with the fact that perceptions are 90% of reality."

Even leading a company with over a century a proven excellence doesn't avert this fate. As Cheryl McKissack describes,

"I deal with it every day. The problem is, a lot of times, clients don't see it. Because they're so used to doing business with people who look like them, they don't realize that they are prejudiced to people

137

who don't. Just last week, I was with one of my good clients, an Ivy League College, we're doing some construction work for them, and their project manager treats my project manager with complete disrespect. And it just so happens that in the building where we're doing our build out, there's also [another construction firm] working on some of the structural renovations of the building. So [the other firm] is a large white firm, and the project manager just gives them leeway to do anything. So if they have to come on our floor to do something, and they get everything dusty and dirty, she will blame us and never turn to [the other company] and even ask the question. To the point where we had to videotape it to prove who was doing what. Now, this whole thing has culminated to where I need to now sit down with the head guy of construction. So last week I'm doing that, and I just tell him, 'This may not be your experience, and this may not be happening on this project, but my experience is that as an African-American firm, we always have to prove we are of quality and that we are as good as the large majority firm.' And he laughed, and he said, 'Oh no, that's not happening here.' But I found out the next day, he was all over this woman and asked her, 'Is it because they're a minority-owned firm?' So I just tell them now. That's part of maturity and getting older; you can just say certain things and be comfortable with it. And I'm just there. I just tell them."

Perceptions of inferiority, though, are not only found in interracial dynamics. Unfortunately, even within the Black community, these assumptions can be wielded against our own. Once again, Cheryl shares an experience that unfortunately, could be described as nothing less than a prime example of a case of Black on Black inferiority complex. But just as is the case when dealing with the issue from those external to the community, casting a mirror to unfair treatment is often the best prescription for change.

"The Studio Museum, which is a Black Museum on 125th Street, they have wealthy Black Board Members. They're doing an $80 million museum in Harlem, where I have a second office on 125th St. and they didn't even invite us to put in a proposal.

So we can be just as prejudiced. I sent out so many e-mails, and they heard from people all over the country. How could you put out an RFP [Request for Proposals] for a Black museum and not invite any Black architects or contractors? Is that ridiculous? I sent them the MLK memorial [RFP]. I sent them the [Smithsonian] African American Museum [RFP]. George Lucus is going to do his museum. He has Melanie heading it up, and they're saying they're going to do all minority firms. So what happened to the Studio Museum? I called everybody because they should be embarrassed. So we deal with it not only from Whites, and Hispanics, and Asians, we deal with it from Blacks as well. What I do, is I bring it to the forefront. I have nothing to lose. So, I told him, I work in Harlem. I protect all the White firms up here from the community picketing them every day. What's it going to look like when they picket you?"

While Cheryl's push-back ultimately landed her the contract, the challenge she faced is not an isolated experience. In fact, for Black women, and particularly young Black women, many have felt the cruelest of all stings—rejection by faces that look just like theirs. Aneisia Williams laments,

"I'm about the work. I'm about really empowering women; really about helping my sisters. But I've had the most hurt by Black women over forty. Women who are upset with where they are. And it's the jealousy about, how'd you get here? You're not old enough! The other women will help me. But as Black women, they will block in a New York heartbeat. We could be so powerful for each other. But I still try."

Cheryl agrees that somewhere along the path, there is a generational disconnect. From her perspective, it all boils down to an identity problem.

"The younger women don't identify with the older women and vice versa. We have to find some connection where the two can meet. I have to see in that young person, something about them that I want to identify myself with."

"It's a work ethic, which I don't know if we're going to get with the younger generation. It's a different world. So we have to accept that, and it's sometimes hard for us to accept because we had to earn our way. When I started working, even though the hours were 9 to 5, I was there 7 to 7. We write thank you notes, and language means something to us. They send a text, and they have half the words there. And you send a letter, and they won't open it. Listen, I have to go to the hairdresser every six weeks to get my touch ups, and you got the nerve to be natural? Our standard was, 'you have to sacrifice.' They don't know why they should..."

Despite these differences, Cheryl agrees, at the end of the day, we need each other.

"We need more women out there that are leading, that are entrepreneurs. The more we have out there looking like us, the more opportunities we have as a group."

Indeed.

It's unfortunate, though, that as Black women our fight for legitimacy as entrepreneurs are fights we seem destined to experience from every direction. From those who doubt our competency because of our race, to those who underestimate our ability because of our gender. But perhaps the deepest cut of all are those we plunge deep into one another. This generational rift is real. It's deep. And unfortunately, it persists.

What's particularly disturbing is that it exists among a group that should know better. We know what it feels like to be excluded, yet we exclude. We know what it feels like to be devalued, yet we devalue our own. And what's most disturbing is that we know what it feels like to be told over and over again that we must wait for a turn at fairness that never seems to come our way. Yet, too often, when we wield the strings of power, for too many of us, it's as if the goal is to hold on to that power to the very end, instead of broadening its reach such that the next generation might continue to advance rather than needlessly start from ground zero time and time again. Only when we pass the baton, willingly and enthusiastically, with experiential knowledge and critical connections generously shared, will we finally have the capacity to reach our greatest potential, not only as business owners, but throughout our power-dynamic as exceptional Black women.

The Power of Prioritizing You

As you embark upon your entrepreneurial journey, keep in mind that one of the easiest things to lose sight of along the way is you. When you make the choice to make a living based on doing what you love, you will soon learn that building a business is not limited to "normal" business hours, or even confined within the boundaries of the typical five-day-work-week. If you allow it, your business can easily take over every aspect of your life. But what good is any "success" you may acquire if it comes at the price of running yourself into the ground to achieve it? And what exactly are you working for, if you can't within the midst of it all, enjoy the life you live today, and not just the one you hope to eventually experience, one day, some day, at some indefinite moment in time?

You need you. As does your business and all of those who love you and whom you love. To live your best life now, weave in the discipline of self-investment and have that become a ritualized part of your daily experience.

Self-investment, of course, comes in many different forms, each as important as the other. It relates to how you treat you, physically, mentally, and spiritually each day. Do you take the time to exercise regularly? Do you feed your spirit through prayer or meditation? Do you honor your mental health by connecting with others in a healthy way, sharing your challenges and burdens, and making space for joy and laughter as a regular part of your life? Do you also feed your mind consistently by consuming books like this one and investing in coaching and other personal and professional development experiences that will ultimately pay you back in dividends by reducing the stress associated with having to figure it all out on your own? If you answered no to any of these questions, it's time to make some adjustments. It's time for you, to prioritize you.

Exceptional Black Woman Vision & Action Guide

1. To create a business that is both destined for success and one that creates a life that you truly enjoy, you must determine the nexus point between what you love and a pre-existing need in the marketplace. What problem(s) can be solved by your product, skills, talents, or expertise? What needs or desires can you fulfill in a particularly compelling or exceptional way?

2. One of the most effective ways to grow your business is through the art of networking. How diverse is your network? And in what ways do you regularly leverage it for sales appointments or other revenue generating activities? Moving forward, what will you do on a consistent basis to not only grow your network but also, to monetize it?

3. Do you need to put you on your to do list? What type of self-investments do you need to make to maximize the success of your business without sacrificing the rest of your life in the process?

PART III
Create a Life You Love

CHAPTER 7

On Love, Life, and Having it All

❝ Your heart will tell you a lot. Your mind will follow. But you have to dig deep and go with your gut. Listen to your heart. And use your mind to formulate the plan. ❞

—Karie Conner
Nike Sales Director

D ivorce was the best thing that ever happened to me. I say that not because I don't believe in love, or as a not-so-veiled attempt to disparage the very idea of marriage. I say that with no ill will or malice aimed at my former husband, the father of my children, and my lifelong friend. I say that because divorce awakened me to the fierce urgency of loving me.

Truth be told, I spent far too many years living a half-life. A life with a career and two adorable children. But also one that included a relationship which had devolved into utter failure. Still, I wore the mask. To the outside world, everything appeared, or so I thought, "normal." I smiled. I laughed. I did what I had to do. But inside, I was dying.

It took a decade of personal unhappiness for me to finally get to the point in my life in which I gave myself permission to prioritize my own joy. It's not that I didn't love myself. It's not that I didn't think I was worthy. It's just that over time, any unhealthy situation that you allow to continue will eventually lull you into a sense of numbness. It will lead you to believe that you don't really need that one most basic, yet precious element of life—joy.

145

Looking back now, I can say with certainty that I spent the better part of my young adulthood in nothing less than a state of suspended animation. I made the mistake of prioritizing pride, other people's judgments, the hustle and bustle of daily responsibilities, and most importantly, fear of what change would mean in my children's lives, in exchange for personal happiness. In focusing all of my energy externally, I sacrificed my inner peace. I was alive, but I wasn't truly living. Hear me Sistahs, nothing, and no one, is worth that price. The day I finally left, with just my boys and what I could fit in the back of my SUV in tow, I began to live again. The day I left, I found my joy.

My boys are now happy, healthy, and well-adjusted young men who have quite smoothly transitioned from one family unit to the practice of dual parenting. My biggest fear, as is the case with most fears, proved to be significantly worse than reality. In fact, my oldest son confessed to me one day that he was happy I left. Noticing my perplexed expression, he continued, "I knew you weren't happy." All those years I wore that mask, thinking I was shielding him and his brother from my personal despair. Ultimately, it was all for not. My mask, it seemed, had significant cracks. Cracks that maybe only a child's love could see. In the end, what my son wanted most was a mother who was happy. The day I prioritized my own joy, was the day I gave him the gift he'd waited years to receive.

You CAN Have it All

It may seem strange to suggest that divorce awakened me to the process that is required to "have it all," but for me, it clearly served that purpose. Of course, I don't recommend it as the ideal path to awakening. In fact, it's my hope that you'll learn from my mistakes, make wise decisions about what you want and need in your life and take a more direct route to that ultimate destination known as "holistic success."

Perhaps the biggest barrier that most face along this path is the outright rejection that holistic success is even a possibility. Most people will tell you, "having it all" is a myth. Some will even suggest that it's an unattainable misogynistic aspiration dangled before women in order to produce undue stress, emotional baggage, and a feeling of inadequacy. As a result of these two overarching narratives, in recent years, the mere thought of having it all has been much maligned and actively rejected. "You can't have it all," is now a common mantra, not only in broader culture, but most importantly, in most of our own minds. If you've fully bought into that notion, let me tell, you've already lost.

Here's the truth. You *already* have it all. The question is, what does your "all" look like? Does it include a career that is free of persistent roadblocks along the way, or, at least, one that is aligned with your passions and greatest ambitions? Does it consist of loving and supportive personal relationships that produce a home environment that provides a sense of peace, a safe space for personal reflection, and a source of deep restoration and renewal? And does it include regular "you" time that feeds your spirit, exercises your talents and nurtures your dreams?

If you answered no to any of these questions, then it's time to get serious about proactively creating a life that is reflective of your greatest desires. It's time to embrace the full breadth of your potential. It's time to finally become ALL of who you were really meant to be.

Know this—true success *requires* holistic success. It encompasses the integration of a home-life and a work-life that pulls together that which you value most into one seamless existence. But the harsh reality is, few of us put the same level of attention and *intention* into our personal lives that we dedicate reflexively to our professional lives.

As someone who leads or aspires to leadership, one thing's for sure—you're a high achiever. You're someone who develops and makes real high expectations. And as such, you understand and implement discipline, sacrifice, focus, and hard work into whatever it is that you do professionally. You know, perhaps better than anyone that the secret sauce to success is to do. Not to pontificate, not to make excuses, not to allow yourself to be pacified by minimized dreams, but to quite literally *find a way* to produce results. And so when your mind is fixed on an aspiration, you assess the situation at hand, develop goals and timetables around the results you seek to achieve, and then you surround yourself with the best team possible to make it happen. In the end, you understand that success takes work. There are no unicorns, pixie dust, or magical incantations that are responsible for the success you've already created or for that to which you aspire. And because you understand this concept, you are willing to pay the price necessary to achieve the results you enjoy.

But to make the shift from mere career success to creating a holistic life you love, you've got to let go of the fairytale that happily ever after is an effortless endeavor. While it's true that creating the home-life of your dreams shouldn't feel like "work," it doesn't just magically occur either. Instead, it's a planned endeavor, structured with specific activity and implemented through the habits of action, assessment, revision, and then more action, all along the way. In a word, it's a process. But there is no process more worthy of you undertaking than one that will result in a life you love, full of joy, contentment, peace and possibility. You are worth the investment. You are worth the effort. You are worth the work.

When I guide clients through the process of developing their Holistic Success Blueprint™ —a personalized strategic plan that helps women successfully create and integrate a personal and professional life they love, I always have them begin by getting very clear about what they want. What is their ideal life? What are those things that are necessary to bring them joy? What are their non-starters? This is not a throw-away task. It's not something you leave to knee-jerk reactions. Instead, you must allow yourself the time and space for deep reflection. I suggest you block off a full day, or, at least, several hours for personal assessment, goal delineation and then brainstorming around the best path to get there. However, truth be told, this is one task that is best completed with the inclusion of an outsider's eye. We each have blind spots when it comes to self-assessment. Ever notice that you might have the ability to give great advice to a friend, yet have difficulty applying that same logic to your own circumstances? It's because as an external observer, you're able to assess situations objectively. You can see and highlight strengths that your friend may believe are merely ordinary or might be completely invisible to her altogether. You're able to easily devise approaches to overcoming challenges that seem almost commonsensical to you, but was completely off her radar screen. It's that outsider's perspective, that's key to making the most of this activity. Log on to *www.blackwomenlead.com* to download your free Holistic Success Blueprint and get information on how best to apply this tool to your life. Keep in mind, though, seamless and satisfying work/life integration doesn't happen overnight. But when it does, it's the most rewarding way imaginable to live your life.

Dr. Julianne Malveaux, President Emerita of Bennett College and Dr. Jane Smith, Vice President for College Relations for Spelman, each have very specific and enlightening advice on how to go about the task of building a life you love. For Dr. Malveaux, it all begins with understanding that life is an evolutionary process. And as such, allow yourself the freedom to invent and reinvent yourself as you traverse the path that best fits your needs at any particular point in time.

She advises,

> *"Know yourself. Know that you're a work in progress. So anytime you make a plan, make space for that plan to change. There is nothing worse than welding yourself to a plan that you don't like anymore. [You] should know something of what you want. Stay in touch with yourself. If you know for sure that you want kids for example, then plan for it. If it's nonnegotiable, then fit it in. Figure out what you must have. If it's children, then go get him. If it's a partner, then go get him. Every day, think what would you do if you knew it was your best day? Every day, do something on that list."*

Like Dr. Malveaux, Dr. Smith believes lists are a critical part of being strategic about how you create an actionable plan for creating your best life. For her, it's all about the process of journaling, but not the traditional way. Journaling via a collection of lists that allow her to prioritize and envision the future she will eventually create. She explains,

> *"You have to have your lists. You have to have your thoughts. I journal lists (not narratives). I don't know a day that I'm not*

149

working with a list. Then you have choices. Like, I'm about to come into a little money, and I know how I'm going to use it because I know from lists what I want vs. what I need. I'll make choices appropriate to the money that I'll be coming into. I have been making lists and making choices all my life. That's the reason I think I have the perfect life, because I chose it. I chose it after thinking through it. I journaled, made choices, and the perfect life is what I've created."

On Black Love

For many, the perfect life is not complete without the perfect partner. But for years, the love lives of Black women have, in many ways, become the fodder of media hype and a profitable fixation of all manner of pseudo-relationship experts. Seizing on a 2009 Yale study which concluded that 42% of Black women have never been married—double the percentage associated with white women—countless media reports and relationship books have not only exploited fears of perpetual loneliness but have used them quite effectively, as a not so subtle marketing ploy. Subsequent research, however, has shown that the entire basis of this trend was built on significantly flawed analysis. Professors Ivory A. Toldson and Bryant Marks of Howard University and Morehouse College respectively, analyzed the same dataset and found that in the original study, the issue is not so much that Black women don't marry, we just tend to marry later in life. Unlike the original study which included women as young as 18 years of age, Toldson and Mark's analysis looked at Black women 35 and older. When examining this group specifically, the percentage of Black women who never married fell to only 25%. As such, fully 75% of Black women were found to ultimately tie the knot.[71]

Still, for many of us, it's this one component that seems to be the most challenging to master. As high-achieving women, our success, at times, can make our love choices that much more complicated to make. Roslyn Brock, Chair of the Board of the NAACP, reflects on her challenges in this most personal of areas.

"I've been widowed for 19 years. Met my husband at the NAACP. He was the Director of Economic Development and I was a Youth Board Member. We were married almost three years. He died tragically at 38. You never think you're going to be a widow at 30. My whole world changed. Over the years, I've met really incredible men, but our men are sometimes threatened by our success or what comes with it. And so that has been a challenge for me. My mother taught me, you don't have to compromise, to be recognized. And so, it's a lonely place. Because so many women who are high-achievers, —the most accomplished women, often, we outgrow our men. And I'm one who doesn't require that he has to have a certain degree. I just want him to be strong in the spirit, have a belief in God, family, and community. [Someone who] wants to give something back and loves me for who I am. I want to be in a situation where I can support him, and likewise, he will support me. And I'm still, I'm waiting to be found. There's a higher standard for women in leadership who are unattached. You can't go to public functions with a different man every time. And so, I live my life in a bubble, with a small circle of friends with whom I can let my hair down and live."

Dr. Maya Rockeymoore, President of Global Policy Solutions and wife of U. S. Congressman Elijah Cummings admits, for high-achieving women, the stakes are indeed high. And so, she was very intentional about her decision in choosing a life partner. In short, she took her time. It's not that she didn't have options, but she knew quite firmly the kind of person she wanted and needed. And so, she was intentional about making a decision that was right for her. In providing advice to others she warns:

"This is one of the most important decisions you will make in your lifetime. You have to find someone who isn't threatened by your intelligence, who is supportive of all aspects of your being, and someone whom you can respect as well. There has to be a balanced level of respect. Pay attention to any red flags that would suggest that this person isn't supportive of your being complete. Finding that

person is difficult, but it can be done. This has to be one of the most clear-headed decisions you make in your lifetime."

Clear headed decisions are key. And as Baltimore Mayor, Stephanie Rawlings-Blake advises, a key component of making that right decision, is opening yourself up to the right person that can come to know and fall in love with the real you. As she puts it,

"Finding somebody that loves you, and not your representative, but you, is key. And that, for me, is someone who loves you at your best and at your worst. And be okay with both of those things. Someone who loves you and respects you and is willing to get married and stay married."

Still, Mayor Blake acknowledges that finding that person means you need to actively put yourself out there, perhaps in new ways, to find the mate that's best for you.

"We are late to the game as far as opening ourselves up to different possibilities. People all over the world are dating outside of their race. It is the norm; it's not the exception. And we are late to the party as far as it being a natural option for us, as Black women. And then too, we've listed ourselves out of options. It has to be somebody that's college educated, it has to be somebody that's making this much money, it has to be someone who belongs to this fraternity, it has to be someone who goes to this church, it has to be...and you know, once you get all those things, you're down to two people, and they're both married!"

"And I've also experienced very ambitious women who are ambitious professionally, and not willing to put that same effort into finding a life partner. Like everything else in life, they're willing to work for except finding a man. Which I don't think makes a whole lot of sense. I remember years ago talking to a girlfriend, very ambitious, very smart, a go-getter, and she was talking about, 'I just can't find a guy.' And I started listing, you should go here, and you should go here, and you should go here...and she said, 'Oh, I don't do that. I don't go to bars.' I'm

like, okay, what about the gym? You can find guys at the gym and guys that share your interest in working out. And she's like, 'Uhm, Uhm. When I go to the gym, I'm working out, I'm not thinking about...' I was like, okay. God is going to send Mr. Right right to your front door. That's what's going to happen. It was like it was something dirty or wrong about being ambitious in your relationships. Like everything else you're supposed to work for, but a guy is supposed to fall in your lap...when you're in sweats and no make-up at the Home Depot."

Like Mayor Blake, Kelly Brinkley, COO of the Capital Area United Way believes anyone can find a mate—that is, if they're willing to place themselves in the best environments to be found. She shared,

"I work out a lot. I tell my Black friends, if you go in Rock Creek Park with a dog, you will get five dates before you leave. Go to a cycling club. Change up where you go meet people, and you will be shocked and amazed with all the guys in there."

"When I met my husband, I was in a running club in Atlanta, and it was thirty men and three women. It was lawyers and doctors. Go hiking, all those things. A ton of guys. When we were in Charlotte, my girlfriend and I decided we wanted to do a white water rafting class, and we were the only two Black women at the facility. I'm like get out of the church! There's nothing there! Triathalon training. Same thing. The guys are in great shape. They love women who are in great shape, and they're so few of us. You got to do something but be in church!"

Still, when it comes to finding a man, not just anyone will do. As Kelly acknowledges, there are some basic qualities that make for a great life partner.

"Look for someone who's kind. Look for someone who believes in taking care of his family. I like to say that even though my husband is a professional, I know that if he lost his job tomorrow, he'd be slinging bags at the airport; he'd be delivering mail on the

weekends. Being with someone who really believes in taking care of his family no matter what, takes so much pressure off. I think I got that from my dad because he was such a provider. No matter the title, look for a kind provider."

Vanessa Cooksey, Sr. Vice-President of Community Affairs at Wells Fargo Advisors proves that love can be found anywhere, but sometimes, only if you're willing to make the first move. She shared,

"I met my husband on an airplane. I thought he was cute. I sat one row ahead of him, in the event he wanted to say something to me, I could hear him. But he didn't say anything. It was a day trip, so coming back that day, I saw him sitting in the gate area. And I rarely see the same person twice, and I knew it was him. So I walked over to him and I said, "I think I'm supposed to know you." And he said, "What's your name?" "And I told him. We sat together on the plane and we've been together, literally, ever since that day."

As Vanessa's experience proves, sometimes love comes to those who not only wait, but recognizes and acts on opportunity. Who knows, had she not had the courage to approach her future husband, their love, and their young son, might have never had the chance to be.

For Michele McNeal, National President of 100 Black Women of America, luck in love came the second time around. After a failed first marriage, when she began thinking about what was really important in her future partner, she got very clear on what her priority was and what it was not.

"This is my second marriage. I had a lot of criteria for my first husband. I wanted him tall, I wanted him to be good-looking because I wanted all of my children to be good looking and I got all of those things. I got a good-looking husband and I got great-looking children. But my husband didn't turn out to be the man that I needed him to be."

*"When I separated and divorced, I knew I enjoyed being married and wanted to be married again. I was telling my mother and my sister one day, I'm not worried about it. I know I'll find another husband, and I don't care if he's on a cane and walks funny and with a bald head, as long as he's good to me and good to my children, that's all that matters to me. So I recognized then that my criteria had changed. So what I really needed was somebody who was supportive of me and loved me and loved my children, because we were a package at that point. I remember as I started dating my now husband, and we pulled up at my parents' house, we heard laughing immediately. And he said, I wonder what they're laughing about. And I looked at him and said, I probably already know. When I got to the front door, they looked at me, and they were still falling out laughing. And I said, 'you know all of you are wrong.' And so, he really wanted to know what they were laughing about, and so my sister said, I'm going to tell you. And she told him what I said. 'She said she was going to find one that was bald, or walked crooked, or walked with a cane. She found it now, didn't she?!' My [future] husband was bald. But I wanted somebody who I could **see the man in**. He was attentive to his mother. He was attentive to his grand-parents. He and his brother took turns and every other month, one of them would go to New Orleans to take their grandparents to the doctor, to make sure their refrigerator was stocked and to take care of their house. I saw a man that was not selfish. A man that knew the importance of family and put family first. And I thought to myself, now I've found a man like my father, and that meant everything to me."*

"I know it's hard for young women. But it's hard for young men as well to find a partner. I keep telling them, don't settle, but look for the right things. Not somebody who is a millionaire, not someone who drives a fancy car. See how they treat their family. Someone who's not selfish. Look deep and stop looking for things that glitter, because it tarnishes over the years. Look for a God-fearing man. Look for someone who is attentive to his father and mother. And absolutely takes care of his children if he

155

has any. Because if he doesn't take care of his own, he's not going to take care of you."

What you need to know without a shadow of a doubt is that you are worthy of love. You are worthy of companionship. And you deserve a life that is reflective of a culture of peace and cooperation in your own home. But here's the kicker. These realities rarely fall into place by happenstance. They come about as a reflection of the actions you take and the choices you make. Make a commitment to prioritize you; your needs, and your desires. In the process, know that even if meeting Mr. Right is something that happens years down the line, or perhaps, not at all, as Janaye Ingram, Immediate Past Executive Director of the National Action Network reminds us, never forget that YOU are enough!

"I would like to be married and have a family, but I have to recognize that I'm enough, and I know that my life is just as complete right now, in this moment, as it would be if I had a husband and kids. I'm not necessarily interested in having a relationship for relationship sake. If you're not someone I can see spending my life with, then I'll probably let that pass because I can focus my energy elsewhere."

"I've had friends of all ages that settle. I had friends in their 40s who married the guy who was the nice guy, but she didn't love him. I can talk about friends now who are doing the same exact thing. They're in their 30s and their clock is ticking-- 'I just need to find somebody!' They're not realizing they're enough. Even if you don't marry this man, you're making a lifetime commitment if you have children with him. It's him and his family. Black women, I'm tired of people trying to diagnose what's wrong with us and why some of us are single. I'm perfectly fine being single. I have an aunt who literally got married in her 80s for the first time. Sometimes it's better to wait until you have the right person. My mom always told me, 'Don't go to the alter trying to alter somebody.'"

As Janaye convincingly conveys, knowing that you are enough, and having the courage to wait for the *right* guy, and not just *a* guy to fit into a preconceived idealized timeline is a critical component of building a life you love. In a world that seemingly in every way conceivable dismisses, disrespects, and devalues Black women, loving you, just as you are, is a revolutionary act. And the real kicker comes when you realize that truly having it all, is merely a reflection of acknowledging, appreciating, and in every conceivable way, falling in love

> "Loving you, just as you are, is a revolutionary act."

with the exceptional being that is you. When that love is so deeply established so as to be woven into how you navigate life on a daily basis, then it becomes easy to value you enough to not settle for good enough, but to be at peace with the wait for the one that is truly worthy. And in the meantime, live life to the fullest!

Motherhood and the Work/Life Conundrum

Whether or not you have the right partner in place, if you have children, you already know that negotiating the dual challenge of motherhood and a demanding career is likely the most difficult and potentially guilt-inducing experience you've ever faced. But even this challenge can be conquered with intentionality and the development of a specific frame from which you define your barometer of success.

For Mayor Blake, she knew from day one, that she would not approach motherhood from a comparative lens. With that fact acknowledged, she went about that task of embracing the motherhood experience from the perspective of how best to create her "all," rather than get caught up in the narrow confines of a singular notion of mothering success.

> *"When I became a mother, I made up my mind that I wasn't going to compare myself to others. I just knew that I would be the best mother I could be. I know in order for me to do what I have to do, I can't have the same "all" as the housewife. I can't have the same "all" as the person who's chosen the traditional 9 to 5. But I do "have it all" in my life. I have a very supportive husband and a precocious child."*

"For me, I was blessed with busy parents. My mom had a very busy career that she took seriously and my dad had a demanding career. But I never felt neglected. That was our life. I don't know if my parents came to all of my [activities], but I knew they loved me. If my mom wasn't there, my aunt was there. We just made it work. For me, if I want to do my job, do it well, and not be in jail, I knew I had to give up on the notion of keeping up with the Jones' and I also had to give up on the notion of being perfect. I wasn't going to be the perfect anything—mother, sister, or boss."

Whether spoken or unspoken, especially as it relates to raising children, it is this pursuit of perfection, which for many working mothers, lead to overwhelming feelings of guilt. And from the perspective of MetricStream CEO, Shellye Archambeau, that's the first thing that you have to let go.

"You have to let go of the guilt. Working moms guilt themselves out of hours of productivity because the world tells you, you should be better. That guilt can just weigh you down. I'm a better mother and a better wife because I'm doing what I want to do. I'm a better person because I'm doing what I want to do. Now, did I see my daughter take her first step? Did I see my son loose his first tooth? No. But you know what, they don't know that! Did I make every game? No. But just like you set expectations at work, make them at home. Tell your child, I can make six games this year and then do that. And then if you make seven, you're a hero, rather than beating yourself up about missing three. Give up the guilt."

The lessons here are clear. First and foremost, actively reject the myth of "perfection." Realize instead that no one is perfect, and any choice you make will be followed by both positive *and* negative consequences. Therefore "perfect" choices are an illusion. They simply don't exist. Understand instead that the most loving thing you can do for yourself and your children is to actively define your own parameters of successful motherhood, without comparisons to others or guilt-inducing notions imposed upon you from the outside world.

Here's what I've learned throughout my motherhood journey. Children need to feel safe. Children need to feel loved. Children need to feel valued. And with honest communication and managed expectations, as long as they have in place an environment in which the basic tenants of love, safety, and value are present, they will have the foundation necessary to not only survive, but to thrive. Don't guilt yourself out of fully enjoying the motherhood experience as *you've* defined it. And don't negate the importance of having your children love you not only as their mother, but also as a role model for achievement in the outside world.

So if you're ready to have it all, know that you can! Today is the day to begin your new path forward. Today is the day to begin the purposeful journey toward *your* all—a holistic life you absolutely love.

Exceptional Black Woman Vision & Action Guide

1. If you could wave a magic wand and have your ideal life tomorrow, what would it look like? In each area of your life, without limitations on your dreams, what do you *really* want?

2. Have you found your ideal partner? If not, what three things do you commit to doing now, to expand the likelihood of meeting someone new? If so, what do you commit to doing regularly in order to keep your relationship strong?

3. What three things do you commit to doing now that prioritize you? Take a moment to put you on your to-do list. Make time to prioritize your joy.

   1.

   2.

   3.

CHAPTER 8

Step into Your Greatness

❝ We need to ask ourselves, 'Why can't I?' instead of saying why I can't. Time waits for no one. So take the limits off your life and believe you are as power-ful as you truly are. ❞

—Natalie Cofield
Founder, Walker's Legacy

Many years ago, I ran across, quite accidentally, a truly amazing medical fact. I found that among the tiniest of premature infants, it is Black girls who are far and away the most likely to live. Among babies weighing only two pounds, roughly the same weight as a quart of milk, Black baby girls are fully twice as likely to survive as White baby boys.[72]

As I absorbed this reality, it came to mind that perhaps from the very beginning, as Black women, we are born fighters. We come to this Earth determined to make a way in a world that on many accounts, will attempt to push us to the periphery. Maybe in prepa-ration for the struggle to come, the seemingly innate strength we carry from infancy serves as a source of sustenance as we traverse our individual paths throughout childhood and ultimately, into the full breadth of Black womanhood.

Now I know that when you get caught up in the daily bustle of life, it's not always easy to remember the strength that was born within you. It's not always easy to remember all of who you truly are. In fact, I would say, that more often than not, it's easier to slip into the lie of inadequacy than to truly believe you are the powerful being that you were in fact born to be.

Every day, especially as Black women, it seems all of who we are is under assault. Our intelligence goes routinely unacknowledged, our contributions are minimized, our beauty is questioned; and our strength is often maligned as either unduly intimidating or as an unflattering counterpoint to our femininity. And even in our most intimate space—our love lives—that which should be private has now been turned into a multi-million dollar industry by those who have found a source of profitability in propagating the lie that as Black women, we are somehow unworthy of love.

I challenge you to see each of these acts for what they truly are—an assault on your dignity and the full-breadth of your humanity. And I implore you to reject those lies and instead, embrace the greatness that lives within you. The greatness, to which you are its rightful heir. The greatness that indeed was there, from the start.

Know that for you to build a life worthy of all of who you are and reflective of both your boldest ambitions and greatest potential, you must become intimately familiar with the full magnificence of you. And then you must engage in the daily task of protecting it against all who would even for one split second, doubt its existence.

I need you to remember that you are exceptional. And as such, you are not only worthy of your boldest ambitions, you are uniquely equipped to make those aspirations real. Know that your dreams are but a reflection of your unique purpose. And so in committing to the daily actions necessary to realize those dreams, you will not only be actively creating a life you'll love, simultaneously, you'll also be creating a better future for us all.

The fact of the matter is, the world needs you. It needs your brilliance and your contributions in every way imaginable. From the streets to the C-Suites, this planet needs the perspectives, experiences, and unique genius that only Black women bring to bear. We need all that you have to offer. And we need it with a sense of urgency that cannot be overstated.

You needn't wait for permission to put in motion the specific actions necessary for you to become the leader you were born to be.

The baton has been passed.

The future is yours.

Now is the time to step into your greatness. Now is the time to be the *Exceptional Black Woman* you've always been, but was never allowed to fully be.

Now's **your** time, to lead.

Exceptional Black Woman Vision & Action Guide

1. Allowing yourself a moment to step away from the habit of humility, take a few minutes to list five of your most exceptional characteristics. In other words, what makes you special?

   1.

   2.

   3.

   4.

   5.

2. Reflecting on the above traits, in what ways do they align with your deepest aspirations? What clues can you take from this alignment as to what may be your ultimate purpose in life?

3. How do you intend to own and fully step into your greatness? Specifically, what actions will you take from this day forward, in order to be all that you were truly meant to be?

About Dr. Avis

Dr. Avis Jones-DeWeever is a Career Reinvention Strategist, Diversity Consultant, and Women's Empowerment Expert. She's the Founder of the *Exceptional Leadership Institute for Women*, a global personal and professional development firm that helps established and aspiring entrepreneurs and executives experience accelerated success while building a holistic life they love. She's also the President of *Incite Unlimited*, a Washington, DC-based boutique consulting firm specializing in diversity consulting, communications strategy and the development and implementation of impactful research.

Dr. Avis formerly served as the youngest ever Executive Director of the **National Council of Negro Women**, a historic membership organization touching the lives of over four million women of African descent worldwide. She's had the honor of being the Keynote Speaker to the Inaugural **President of the United States' Young African Leaders Summit** and was a Featured Speaker before the **World Bank**. She currently conducts workshops and trainings on women's career and entrepreneurial success on behalf of **U.S. Embassies** across the globe and helps **corporations** better design and implement strategies to maximize the power of diversity and inclusion at work as well as for the marketplace of today and tomorrow. For individuals, Dr. Avis coaches one-on-one, in small groups, and through on-line courses in order to help her clients *Master the Art of the Career Shift*. In so doing, she helps women shift their careers in three distinct areas: (1) ascending to leadership within their current professional space; (2) safely and effectively transitioning to a new career; or (3) making the ultimate shift, from employee to successful entrepreneur.

Find Dr. Avis regularly as a Contributor to TV One's NewsOne Now with Roland Martin, PBS' To the Contrary, Sirius XM Radio's The Agenda, and the Huffington Post. To learn more, log on to: www.avisjonesdeweever.com.

Need a Dynamic Speaker for an Upcoming Event?

Dr. Avis speaks regularly at corporations, colleges, major conferences, and events within the U.S. and throughout the world. To inquire about her availability, please reach out to **concierge@avisjonesdeweever .com** or find out more at www.avisjonesdeweever.com.

Exceptional Leadership Institute for Women

Live Workshops and Trainings

Intersectional Intelligence™

You may know about Cultural Competence. You may even understand the power of Gender Intelligence. But have you considered how your company can maximize the unique assets that Women of Color bring? Learn how the keen insights of this specific demographic can give your organization the competitive edge in both today's emerging markets and among tomorrow's rising American majority. Understand how to develop effective recruitment and retention strategies that work for this specific demographic and gain insight on how to create an organizational culture that not only understands the value of diversity and inclusion, but leverages it to produce powerful results.

Business Mastery

Do you dream of starting your own business, but don't know where to begin? This in-depth, interactive workshop will teach you how to go from concept, to clarity, to successful entrepreneurial action!

Excellence at the Intersection: Leadership Success Strategies for Women of Color

The formula for leadership success for Women of Color is significantly more complicated than merely leaning in. In this workshop, find out how to successfully navigate the intersecting challenges of race and gender in the workplace, and ultimately, take your place at the top!

The Group Coaching Experience

The C-Suite Society™

Are you ready for that next promotion? If so, this group coaching experience is just what you need to shift your career into high gear. Here you'll learn a wide range of critical skills essential for career ascension. From growing a network that *works*, to getting noticed *and* getting credit for all the hard work you do, to even getting a handle on negotiation strategies that maximize your bottom line, the C-Suite Society™ will get you prepared, positioned, and ready to propel forward to your next-level of success!

Career Shift Network™

Have you fallen out of love with what you do? Would you like to change lanes all together and transition into something entirely new? If so, this group-coaching experience was developed just for you! By joining the Career Shift Network™ you'll receive the guidance, support, information, and accountability necessary to safely and successfully transition into a new career you'll love.

Monetize My Passion Masterclass™

Do you have a passion you'd like to get out of your heart and into the world in a profitable way? If so, this 4-week on-line digital Masterclass will give you the critical information you need to get your business idea into the world safely, effectively, and of course, profitably! Each week, you'll receive succinct video-training modules sharing proven techniques for business success. Each module is supplemented by a downloadable workbook in which you can apply the principles shared to your specific business idea. You'll also have access to four weekly live Q & A Calls with Dr. Avis to answer any questions and receive direct feedback on how to most effectively turn your passion into profits!

Launch My Profitable Business Mastermind™

Perhaps the most difficult and critical stage of the entrepreneurial journey occurs in the start-up phase. Those first few months can either provide a strong foundation for growth, or be a shaky beginning leading to an untimely end. This Mastermind Experience was specifically developed to guide you through the critical launch stage of your business. You'll receive instruction directly from Dr. Avis as well as a wide range of expert faculty in order to ensure you're equipped with the information you need to start your business off right! You'll also get access to a supportive community of like-minded budding entrepreneurs, all seeking to turn their dreams into a thriving new and profitable reality. Altogether, you'll get valuable information, accountability, and access to a broad network of experts and pace-setting peers, which together, provide the perfect environment for accelerated business success.

To be added to the waiting list, get more information about any of the above-mentioned group coaching experiences, or to learn how you can receive Private VIP Coaching from Dr. Avis, e-mail us at: concierge@ avisjonesdeweever.com

Acknowledgements

There are not enough words to express my level of gratitude for those who have supported me throughout the life of this project. More than two years and seventy interviews in the making, this is an effort that literally would not have been possible without a village of supporters. In fact, there are so many people to thank that I run the risk of leaving out a few. Please forgive me if that is indeed the case, but I could not bring this book to its conclusion without specifically recognizing the following cadre of family, friends, colleagues, and stellar professionals:

My amazing parents, Mr. Angelo Jones and Mrs. Georgianna Reid Jones. You are, frankly, more than parents to me. You have each been an amazing source of inspiration, wisdom, encouragement and love since the day I first appeared on this planet. I am so proud of each of you. Not only for your ground-breaking individual professional accomplishments, but also for the love that you share and generously provide to so many. Everything that I am and aspire to be, spawns from the lessons and inspiration I have been fortunate enough to take from you. So proud to be your baby.

To my incredible sons, Aidan and Guy. Thank you both for your patience and support throughout this process. Specifically, Guy, your help in organizing the hundreds of pages of interview transcripts was absolutely invaluable. Without complaint or hesitation, you pitched in to help precisely when I needed it most, and I will be forever grateful. Aidan, thank you so much for entertaining Boo, our beloved dog, and helping to make sure all was quiet on the home front during all those interviews. Also, thanks for never complaining about maybe one too many pizza deliveries at the end! I couldn't have asked for more supportive, helpful and loving sons. I love you both to pieces!

To my sister Angela and niece, Ayana, thank you both for always being a critical source of encouragement and support not only throughout this journey but throughout all of those amazing adventures life happened to bring our way.

To my amazing Assistant, Sandra Hart. Your insights and stellar research skills were an absolutely essential component to the completion of this work. Thank you, thank you, thank you for being the Exceptional Young Black Woman that you are!

To my incredible book consultant, Tressa Smallwood. Girl, you are the truth! You and your team were just the magic ingredient I needed to ultimately make everything come together with an air of professionalism and excellence. Thank you for believing in my vision and helping to bring it to life spectacularly.

And finally, to each and every one of the Exceptional Black Women who generously gave their time and wisdom to this project, please know that even if your words are not specifically quoted in this work, your insights and wisdom were essential to the development of the overarching ideals shared throughout the book. Thank you immensely for investing your brilliance into the next generation of Black women leaders.

Stay Connected...

I'd love to hear about the transformations this book creates in your life. So I invite you to stay in touch! Share your stories of success with me by e-mailing: **concierge@avisjonesdeweever.com**

Also, feel free to connect online through any and all of the following platforms:

Twitter: @sistahscholar
Periscope: @sistahscholar
Instagram: TheRealDr.Avis
Facebook: Dr. Avis Jones-DeWeever
LinkedIn: Avis Jones-DeWeever, Ph.D.
Website: www.avisjonesdeweever.com

Endnotes

1   U.S. Bureau of Labor Statistics. Current Population survey, 2012 Annual Averages. Table 3. "Employment status of the civilian noninstitutional population by age, sex, and race." http://www.bls.gov/cps/cpsaat03.htm

2   U.S. Bureau of Labor Statistics (August 2012). *Labor Force Characteristics by Race and Ethnicity, 2011* (page 3 and Table 10). "Employment and unemployment of families by type of family, race, and Hispanic or Latino ethnicity, 2011 annual averages" (page 34). www.bls.gov/cps/cpsrace2011.pdf

3   Hewlett, Sylvia and Tai Green. July 11, 2015. *Qualified Black Women are Being Held Back from Management.* Harvard Business Review. https://hbr.org/2015/06/qualified-black-women-are-being-held-back-from-management

4   Jessica Faye Carter, *Double Outsiders: How Women of Color Can Succeed in Corporate America,* (Indianapolis: JIST Works. 2007).

5   Catalyst, *Advancing African-American Women in the Workplace: What Managers Need to Know,* (New York: Catalyst, 2004).

6   Hope Yen, *Census: White Majority in U.S. Gone by 2043.* NBC News. June 13, 2013. http://usnews.nbcnews.com/_news/2013/06/13/18934111-census-white-majority-in-us-gone-by-2043?lite

7   Hannes van Rensburg, *Africa is Rising Fast.* Forbes. November 9, 2012. http://www.forbes.com/sites/techonomy/2012/11/09/africa-is-rising-fast/

8   Ellen McGirt, January, 2016. *Leading While Black: Why Race and Culture Matters in the C-Suite.* Fortune.com. http://fortune.com/black-executives-men-c-suite/

9   Valerie Purdie-Vaughns. April 22, 2015. *Why So Few Black Women are Senior Managers in 2015.* Fortune.com. *http://fortune.com/2015/04/22/black-women-leadership-study/*

10 Catalyst, *Advancing African-American Women in the Workplace: What Managers Need to Know,* (New York: Catalyst, 2004).

11 Ibid.

12 Ibid.

13 Ibid.

14 Hewlett, Sylvia Ann and Tai Green. 2014. *Black Women: Ready to Lead.* (New York: Center for Talent Innovation).

15 Gellman, Lindsay. September 30, 2015. The Racial Gap in Mentoring at Work. The Wall Street Journal. http://www.wsj.com/articles/a-racial-gap-in-mentoring-at-work-1443600872

16 Author's calculations based on analyzing the number of women, Blacks, Latinos, and Asian CEOs.

17 Ana Swanson, *The Number of Fortune 500 Companies led by Women is at an AllTime High: 5 Percent.* Washington Post. June 4, 2015.

18 U.S. Department of Education, National Center for Education Statistics. (2012). *The Condition of Education 2012* (NCES 2012-045), Indicator 47.

19 U.S. Department of Education, National Center for Education Statistics. (2012). *The Condition of Education 2012* (NCES 2012-045), Table A-47-2.

20 Zweigenhaft, R. L. & Domhoff, G.W. 2014. *The New CEOs: Women, African American, Latino, and Asian American Leaders of Fortune 500 Companies.* Lanham, MD: Rowman & Littlefield.

21 Ana Swanson, The Number of Fortune 500 Companies led by Women is at an AllTime High: 5 Percent. Washington Post. June 4, 2015

22 Zweigenhaft, R. L. & Domhoff, G.W. 2014. The New CEOs: Women, African American, Latino, and Asian American Leaders of Fortune 500 Companies. Lanham, MD: Rowman & Littlefield.

23 DiversityInc. 2015. *McDonald's CEO to Retire: Black Fortune 500 CEOs Decline by 33% in Past Year.* http://www.diversityinc.com/leadership/mcdonalds-ceo-retire-black-fortune-500-ceos-decline-33-past-year/

24 Tim Wise, *Is Sisterhood Conditional? White Women and the Rollback of Affirmative Action.* 10(3):1-. 26. (January, 1998).

25 Tina Vasquez, Black Women in Business: An Update on Progress. http://theglasshammer.com/2014/02/04/black-women-in-business-an-update-on-progress/

26 Boschma, Janie. February 2, 2016. *Black Consumers Have 'Unprecedented Impact' in 2015.'* The Atlantic. http://www.theatlantic.com/politics/archive/2016/02/black-consumers-have-unprecedented-impact-in-2015/433725/

27 Ibid.

28 Richard Zweigenhaft and G. William Domhoff, *Diversity and the New CEOs,* (The Society Pages, July 5, 2012).

29 Heather Joslyn, *A Man's World: Big Charities Overwhelmingly Run by White Males a Chronicle Survey Finds,* (The Chronicle of Philanthropy, September 17, 2009). https://philanthropy.com/article/A-Mans-World/57099/

30 Ibid. Author's calculations based on the reported results of the Philanthropy 400 Survey.

31 Ibid.

32 American Express Open, The State of Women-Owned Businesses 2015, (New York: American Express Open, 2015).

33 Ibid.

34 Ibid.

35 Alicia Robb, *Access to Capital Among Young Firms, Minority-Owned Firms, Women-Owned Firms, and High Tech Firms.* (San Rafael, CA: Marin Consulting, 2013).

36 O'Brian, Sarah Ashley. Only 88 Tech Start Ups are Run by Black Women. CNN. http://money.cnn.com/2016/02/17/technology/black-women-tech-startups-project-diane/

37 American Express Open, *The State of Women-Owned Businesses 2013,* (New York: American Express Open, 2013).

38 http://www.gmcl.org/maps/national/gender.htm Accessed 2/1/2104

39 Center for the American Woman and Politics. *Women of Color in American Politics,* (New Brunswick, NJ: Center for the American Woman and Politics, Eagleton Institute of Politics, Rutgers University).

40 Kira Sanbonmatsu, Susan J. Carroll, and Debbie Walsh, *Poised to Run: Women's Pathways to the State Legislatures,* (Center for American

Women and Politics, Eagleton Institute of Politics, Rutgers University, 2009).

41 Ibid.

42 Please note that I am characterizing California Attorney General, Kamila Harris, as Black, due to her father's Black Jamaican heritage. She could also be categorized as Multiracial. It is unclear how Attorney General Harris racially self-identifies.

43 Center for the American Woman and Politics. *Women of Color in Elective Office 2015*, (New Brunswick, NJ: Center for the American Woman and Politics, Eagleton Institute of Politics, Rutgers University).

44 Ibid.

45 Ibid. Please note that I am characterizing California Attorney General, Kamila Harris, as Black, due to her Father's Black Jamaican heritage. She could also be categorized as Multiracial. It is unclear how Attorney General Harris racially self-identifies.

46 Robert W. Livingston, *Gender, Race, and Leadership: An Examination of the Challenges Facing Non-prototypical Leaders*, Harvard Business School Research Symposium Gender and Work: Challenging Conventional Wisdom. 2013.

47 Ashleigh Shelby Rosette and Robert W. Livingston, *Failure is Not an Option for Black Women: Effects of Organizational Performance on Leaders with Single vs. Dual Subordinate Identities*, Journal of Experimental Social Psychology, 48(5): 1162-1167.

48 Thomas Fuchs, *The Late, Great American WASP*, The Wall Street Journal, December 23, 2013.

49 Wendy Smooth, *Intersectionality in Electoral Politics, a Mess Worth Making*, Politics and Gender, 3:400-414.

50 The White House. *Remarks by the First Lady at Tuskegee University Commencement Address.* https://www.whitehouse.gov/the-press-office/2015/05/09/remarks-first-lady-tuskegee-university-commencement-address

51 Ibid.

52 Shulevitz, Judith. *The Science of Suffering.* New Republic. November 16, 2014

53 Ibid.

54 United Nations Educational, Scientific, and Cultural Organization. Transatlantic Slave Trade. http://www.unesco.org/new/en/culture/themes/dialogue/the-slave-route/transatlantic-slave-trade/

55 DeGruy, Joy. 2005. Post Traumatic Slave Syndrome: America's Legacy of Enduring Injury and Healing. Portland: Joy DeGruy Publications

56 Shulevitz, Judith. *The Science of Suffering*. New Republic., November 16, 2014

57 DeGruy, Joy. 2005. Post Traumatic Slave Syndrome: America's Legacy of Enduring Injury and Healing. Portland: Joy DeGruy Publications

58 Fox, Maggie. September 15, 2015. *Black Kids Get Less Pain Medication Than White Kids in the ER.* NBC News http://www.nbcnews.com/health/kids-health/black-kids-get-less-pain-medication-white-kids-er-n427056

59 Freeman, Harld. March 13, 2014. Why Black Women Die of Breast Cancer. New York Times. http://www.nytimes.com/2014/03/14/opinion/why-black-women-die-of-cancer.html?_r=0

60 Green, et. al. , September, 2007. Implicit Bias Among Physicians and its Prediction of Thrombolysis Decisions for Black and White Patients. *Journal of General Internal Medicine. Volume 22, Issue 9, pp. 1231-1238.*

61 CDO Insights. August, 2008. *Proven Strategies for Addressing Unconscious Bias in the Workplace.* Volume 2 Issue 5.

62 Yurkiewicz, Ilana. September 23, 2012. Study Shows Gender Bias in Science is Real. Here's Why it Matters. *Scientific American.* http://blogs.scientificamerican.com/unofficial-prognosis/study-shows-gender-bias-in-science-is-real-heres-why-it-matters/

63 Ibid.

64 Purdie-Vaughns, Valerie. April 22, 2015. "Why So Few Black Women are Senior Managers in 2015." Fortune.com. http://fortune.com/2015/04/22/black-women-leadership-study/

65 The Evolutionary Layers of the Human Brain. http://thebrain.mcgill.ca/flash/d/d_05/d_05_cr/d_05_cr_her/d_05_cr_her.html

66 Henneman, Todd. February 9, 2014. You, Biased? No, It's Your Brain. *Workforce*. http://www.workforce.com/articles/20242-you-biased-no-its-your-brain

67 Herbert, Nick. 1994. Elemental Mind: Human Consciousness and the New Physics. Plume.

68 Emerging Technology. August 25, 2009. New Measure of Human Brain Processing Speed. *MIT Technology Review*. http://www.technologyreview.com/view/415041/new-measure-of-human-brain-processing-speed/

69 Ibid.

70 Mariko Chang, *Lifting as We Climb: Women of Color, Wealth, and America's Future*. (Insight Center for Community and Economic Development, 2010).

71 Desmond-Harris, Jenee. August 18, 2011. Myth-busting the Black Marriage Crisis." *The Root*. *http://www.theroot.com/articles/culture/2011/08/black_marriage_good_news_by_the_numbers.html*

72 Morse, Steven B., Samuel S. Wu, Changxing Ma, Mario Ariet, Michael Resnick and Jeffrey Roth. 2006. "Racial and Gender Differences in the Viability of Extremely Low Birth Weight Infants: A Population-Based Study." Pediatrics 117 (1): 106-112.

Made in the USA
Coppell, TX
11 March 2021

51586797R00105